EXTRA-ILLUSTRATED EDITION

∵

VOLUME 45
THE CHRONICLES
OF AMERICA SERIES
ALLEN JOHNSON
EDITOR

GERHARD R. LOMER
CHARLES W. JEFFERYS
ASSISTANT EDITORS

OLIVER H. KELLEY

From a photograph.

THE
AGRARIAN CRUSADE

A CHRONICLE OF
THE FARMER IN POLITICS
BY SOLON J. BUCK

NEW HAVEN: YALE UNIVERSITY PRESS
TORONTO: GLASGOW, BROOK & CO.
LONDON: HUMPHREY MILFORD
OXFORD UNIVERSITY PRESS

1921

PREFACE

RAPID growth accompanied by a somewhat painful readjustment has been one of the leading characteristics of the history of the United States during the last half century. In the West the change has been so swift and spectacular as to approach a complete metamorphosis. With the passing of the frontier has gone something of the old freedom and the old opportunity; and the inevitable change has brought forth inevitable protest, particularly from the agricultural class. Simple farming communities have wakened to find themselves complex industrial regions in which the farmers have frequently lost their former preferred position. The result has been a series of radical agitations on the part of farmers determined to better their lot. These movements have manifested different degrees of coherence and intelligence, but all have had something of the same purpose and spirit, and all may justly be considered as stages of the still unfinished agrarian crusade. This book is an attempt to sketch the course and to reproduce the spirit of that crusade from its inception with the Granger movement, through the Greenback and Populist phases, to a climax in the battle for free silver.

In the preparation of the chapters dealing with Populism I received invaluable assistance from my colleague, Professor Lester B. Shippee of the University of Minnesota; and I am indebted to my wife for aid at every stage of the work, especially in the revision of the manuscript.

SOLON J. BUCK.

MINNESOTA HISTORICAL SOCIETY,
      ST. PAUL.

CONTENTS

ILLUSTRATIONS

THE AGRARIAN CRUSADE

∴

CHAPTER I

THE INCEPTION OF THE GRANGE

WHEN President Johnson authorized the Commissioner of Agriculture, in 1866, to send a clerk in his bureau on a trip through the Southern States to procure "statistical and other information from those States," he could scarcely have foreseen that this trip would lead to a movement among the farmers, which, in varying forms, would affect the political and economic life of the nation for half a century. The clerk selected for this mission, one Oliver Hudson Kelley, was something more than a mere collector of data and compiler of statistics: he was a keen observer and a thinker. Kelley was born in Boston of a good Yankee family that could boast kinship with Oliver Wendell Holmes and Judge Samuel Sewall. At the age of twenty-three

1

he journeyed to Iowa, where he married. Then with his wife he went on to Minnesota, settled in Elk River Township, and acquired some first-hand familiarity with agriculture. At the time of Kelley's service in the agricultural bureau he was forty years old, a man of dignified presence, with a full beard already turning white, the high broad forehead of a philosopher, and the eager eyes of an enthusiast. "An engine with too much steam on all the time" — so one of his friends characterized him; and the abnormal energy which he displayed on the trip through the South justifies the figure.

Kelley had had enough practical experience in agriculture to be sympathetically aware of the difficulties of farm life in the period immediately following the Civil War. Looking at the Southern farmers not as a hostile Northerner would but as a fellow agriculturist, he was struck with the distressing conditions which prevailed. It was not merely the farmers' economic difficulties which he noticed, for such difficulties were to be expected in the South in the adjustment after the great conflict; it was rather their blind disposition to do as their grandfathers had done, their antiquated methods of agriculture, and, most of all, their apathy. Pondering on this attitude, Kelley decided that it was fostered if not caused by the lack of social opportunities which made the existence of the farmer such a drear monotony that he became practically incapable of changing his outlook on life or his attitude toward his work.

Being essentially a man of action, Kelley did not stop with the mere observation of these evils but cast about to find a remedy.   In doing so, he came to the conclusion that a national secret order of farmers resembling the Masonic order, of which he was a member, might serve to bind the farmers together for purposes of social and intellectual advancement.   After he returned from the South, Kelley discussed the plan in Boston with his niece, Miss Carrie Hall, who argued quite sensibly that women should be admitted to full membership in the order, if it was to accomplish the desired ends. Kelley accepted her suggestion and went West to spend the summer in farming and dreaming of his project.   The next year found him again in Washington, but this time as a clerk in the Post Office Department.

During the summer and fall of 1867 Kelley interested some of his associates in his scheme.   As a result seven men — "one fruit grower and six government clerks, equally distributed among the

Post Office, Treasury, and Agricultural Departments" — are usually recognized as the founders of the Patrons of Husbandry, or, as the order is more commonly called, the Grange. These men, all of whom but one had been born on farms, were O. H. Kelley and W. M. Ireland of the Post Office Department, William Saunders and the Reverend A. B. Grosh of the Agricultural Bureau, the Reverend John Trimble and J. R. Thompson of the Treasury Department, and F. M. McDowell, a pomologist of Wayne, New York. Kelley and Ireland planned a ritual for the society; Saunders interested a few farmers at a meeting of the United States Pomological Society in St. Louis in August, and secured the coöperation of McDowell; the other men helped these four in corresponding with interested farmers and in perfecting the ritual. On December 4, 1867, having framed a constitution and adopted the motto *Esto perpetua*, they met and constituted themselves the National Grange of the Patrons of Husbandry. Saunders was to be Master; Thompson, Lecturer; Ireland, Treasurer; and Kelley, Secretary.

It is interesting to note, in view of the subsequent political activity in which the movement for agricultural organization became inevitably involved, that the founders of the Grange looked for advantages to come to the farmer through intellectual and social intercourse, not through political action. Their purpose was "the advancement of agriculture," but they expected that advancement to be an educative rather than a legislative process. It was to that end, for instance, that they provided for a Grange "Lecturer," a man whose business it was to prepare for each meeting a program apart from the prescribed ritual — perhaps a paper read by one of the members or an address by a visiting speaker. With this plan for social and intellectual advancement, then, the founders of the Grange set out to gain members.

During the first four years the order grew slowly, partly because of the mistakes of the founders, partly because of the innate conservatism and suspicion of the average farmer. The first local Grange was organized in Washington. It was made up largely of government clerks and their wives and served less to advance the cause of agriculture than to test the ritual. In February, 1868, Kelley resigned his clerkship in the Post Office Department and turned his whole attention to the organization of the new order. His colleagues, in optimism or irony, voted him a salary of two thousand dollars a year and traveling expenses, to be paid from the receipts of any subordinate Granges he should establish. Thus authorized, Kelley bought a ticket for Harrisburg, and with two dollars and a half in his pocket, started out to work his way to Minnesota by organizing Granges. On his way out he sold four dispensations for the establishment of branch organizations — three for Granges in Harrisburg, Columbus, and Chicago, which came to nothing, and one for a Grange in Fredonia, New York, which was the first regular, active, and permanent local organization. This, it is important to note, was established as a result of correspondence with a farmer of that place, and in by far the smallest town of the four. Kelley seems at first to have made the mistake of attempting to establish the order in the large cities, where it had no native soil in which to grow.

When Kelley revised his plan and began to work from his farm in Minnesota and among neighbors whose main interest was in agriculture, he was more successful. His progress was not, however, so marked as to insure his salary and expenses; in fact, the whole history of these early years represents the hardest kind of struggle against financial difficulties. Later, Kelley wrote of this difficult period: "If all great enterprises, to be permanent, must necessarily start from small beginnings, our Order is all right. Its foundation was laid on *solid nothing* — the rock of poverty — and there is no harder material." At times the persistent secretary found himself unable even to buy postage for his circular letters. His friends at Washington began to lose interest in the work of an order with a treasury "so empty that a five-cent stamp would need an introduction before it would feel at home in it." Their only letters to Kelley during this trying time were written to remind him of bills owed by the order. The total debt was not more than $150, yet neither the Washington members nor Kelley could find funds to liquidate it. "My dear brother," wrote Kelley to Ireland, "you must not swear when the printer comes in. . . . When they come in to 'dun' ask them to take a seat; light your pipe; lean back in a chair, and suggest to them that some plan be adopted to bring in ten or twenty members, and thus furnish funds to pay their bills." A note of $39, in the hands of one Mr. Bean, caused the members in Washington further embarrassment at this time and occasioned a gleam of humor in one of Kelley's letters. Bean's calling on the men at Washington, he wrote, at least reminded them of the absentee, and to be cursed by an old friend was better than to be forgotten. "I suggest," he continued, "that Granges use black and white *Beans* for ballots."

In spite of all his difficulties, Kelley stubbornly continued his endeavor and kept up the fiction of a powerful central order at the capital by circulating photographs of the founders and letters which spoke in glowing terms of the great national organization of the Patrons of Husbandry. "It must be advertised as vigorously as if it were a patent medicine," he said; and to that end he wrote articles for leading agricultural papers, persuaded them to publish the constitution of the Grange, and inserted from time to time press notices which kept the organization before the public eye. In May, 1868, came the first fruits of all this correspondence and advertisement — the establishment of a Grange at Newton, Iowa. In September, the first permanent Grange in Minnesota, the North Star Grange, was established at St. Paul with the assistance of Colonel D. A. Robertson. This gentleman and his associates interested themselves in spreading the order. They revised the Grange circulars to appeal to the farmer's pocketbook, emphasizing the fact that the order offered a means of protection against corporations and opportunities for coöperative buying and selling. This practical appeal was more effective than the previous idealistic propaganda: two additional Granges were established before the end of the year; a state Grange was constituted early in the next year; and by the end of 1869 there were in Minnesota thirty-seven active Granges. In the spring of 1869 Kelley went East and, after visiting the thriving Grange in Fredonia, he made his report at Washington to the members of the National Grange, who listened perfunctorily, passed a few laws, and relapsed into indifference after this first regular annual session.

But however indifferent the members of the National Grange might be as to the fate of the organization they had so irresponsibly fathered, Kelley was zealous and untiring in its behalf. That the founders did not deny their parenthood was enough for him; he returned to his home with high hopes for the future. With the aid of his niece he carried on an indefatigible correspondence which soon brought tangible returns. In October, 1870, Kelley moved his headquarters to Washington. By the end of the year the Order had penetrated nine States of the Union, and correspondence looking to its establishment in seven more States was well under way. Though Granges had been planted as far east as Vermont and New Jersey and as far south as Mississippi and South Carolina, the life of the order as yet centered in Minnesota, Iowa, Wisconsin, Illinois, and Indiana. These were the only States in which, in its four years of activity the Grange had really taken root; in other States only sporadic local Granges sprang up. The method of organization, however, had been found and tested. When a few active subordinate Granges had been established in a State, they convened as a temporary state Grange, the master of which appointed deputies to organize other subordinate Granges throughout the State. The initiation fees, generally three dollars for men and fifty cents for women, paid the expenses of organization — fifteen dollars to the deputy, and not infrequently a small sum to the state Grange. What was left went into the treasury of the local Grange. Thus by the end of 1871 the ways and means of spreading the Grange had been devised. All that was now needed was some impelling motive which should urge the farmers to enter and support the organization.

CHAPTER II

THE decade of the seventies witnessed the subsidence, if not the solution, of a problem which had vexed American history for half a century — the reconciliation of two incompatible social and economic systems, the North and the South. It witnessed at the same time the rise of another great problem, even yet unsolved — the preservation of equality of opportunity, of democracy, economic as well as political, in the face of the rising power and influence of great accumulations and combinations of wealth. Almost before the battle smoke of the Civil War had rolled away, dissatisfaction with prevailing conditions both political and economic began to show itself.

The close of the war naturally found the Republican or Union party in control throughout the North. Branded with the opprobrium of having opposed the conduct of the war, the Democratic party remained impotent for a number of years; and Ulysses S. Grant, the nation's greatest military hero, was easily elected to the presidency on the Republican ticket in 1868. In the latter part of Grant's first term, however, hostility began to manifest itself among the Republicans themselves toward the politicians in control at Washington. Several causes tended to alienate from the President and his advisers the sympathies of many of the less partisan and less prejudiced Republicans throughout the North. Charges of corruption and maladministration were rife and had much foundation in truth. Even if Grant himself was not consciously dishonest in his application of the spoils system and in his willingness to receive reward in return for political favors, he certainly can be justly charged with the disposition to trust too blindly in his friends and to choose men for public office rather because of his personal preferences than because of their qualifications for positions of trust.

Grant's enemies declared, moreover, with considerable truth that the man was a military autocrat, unfit for the highest civil position in a democracy. His high-handed policy in respect to Reconstruction in the South evoked opposition from those

Northern Republicans whose critical sense was not entirely blinded by sectional prejudice and passion. The keener-sighted of the Northerners began to suspect that Reconstruction in the South often amounted to little more than the looting of the governments of the Southern States by the greedy freedmen and the unscrupulous carpetbaggers, with the troops of the United States standing by to protect the looters.   In 1871, under color of necessity arising from the intimidation of voters in a few sections of the South, Congress passed a stringent act, empowering the President to suspend the writ of *habeas corpus* and to use the military at any time to suppress disturbances or attempts to intimidate voters.   This act, in the hands of radicals, gave the carpetbag governments of the Southern States practically unlimited powers.   Any citizens who worked against the existing administrations, however peacefully, might be charged with intimidation of voters and prosecuted under the new act. Thus these radical governments were made practically self-perpetuating.   When their corruption, wastefulness, and inefficiency became evident, many people in the North frankly condemned them and the Federal Government which continued to support them.

This dissatisfaction with the Administration on the part of Republicans and independents came to a head in 1872 in the Liberal-Republican movement. As early as 1870 a group of Republicans in Missouri, disgusted by the excesses of the radicals in that State in the proscription of former Confederate sympathizers, had led a bolt from the party, had nominated B. Gratz Brown for governor, and, with the assistance of the Democrats, had won the election. The real leader of this movement was Senator Carl Schurz, under whose influence the new party in Missouri declared not only for the removal of political disabilities but also for tariff revision and civil service reform and manifested opposition to the alienation of the public domain to private corporations and to all schemes for the repudiation of any part of the national debt. Similar splits in the Republican party took place soon afterwards in other States, and in 1872 the Missouri Liberals called a convention to meet at Cincinnati for the purpose of nominating a candidate for the presidency.

The new party was a coalition of rather diverse elements. Prominent tariff reformers, members of the Free Trade League, such as David A. Wells and Edward L. Godkin of the *Nation*, advocates of civil service reform, of whom Carl Schurz was a leading representative, and especially opponents of the reconstruction measures of the Administration, such as Judge David Davis and Horace Greeley, saw an opportunity to promote their favorite policies through this new party organization.   To these sincere reformers were soon added such disgruntled politicians as A. G. Curtin of Pennsylvania and R. E. Fenton of New York, who sought revenge for the support which the Administration had given to their personal rivals.   The principal bond of union was the common desire to prevent the reëlection of Grant.   The platform adopted by the Cincinnati convention reflected the composition of the party.   Opening with a bitter denunciation of the President, it declared in no uncertain terms for civil service reform and the immediate and complete removal of political disabilities.   On the tariff, however, the party could come to no agreement; the free traders were unable to overcome the opposition of Horace Greeley and his protectionist followers; and the outcome was the reference of the question "to the people in their congressional districts and the decision of Congress."

The leading candidates for nomination for the presidency were Charles Francis Adams, David

Davis, Horace Greeley, Lyman Trumbull, and B. Gratz Brown. From these men, as a result of manipulation, the convention unhappily selected the one least suited to lead the party to victory — Horace Greeley. The only hope of success for the movement was in coöperation with that very Democratic party whose principles, policies, and leaders, Greeley in his editorials had unsparingly condemned for years. His extreme protectionism repelled not only the Democrats but the tariff reformers who had played an important part in the organization of the Liberal Republican party. Conservatives of both parties distrusted him as a man with a dangerous propensity to advocate "isms," a theoretical politician more objectionable than the practical man of machine politics, and far more likely to disturb the existing state of affairs and to overturn the business of the country in his efforts at reform. As the *Nation* expressed it, "Greeley appears to be 'boiled crow' to more of his fellow citizens than any other candidate for office in this or any other age of which we have record."

The regular Republican convention renominated Grant, and the Democrats, as the only chance of victory, swallowed the candidate and the platform of the Liberals. Doubtless Greeley's opposition to

the radical reconstruction measures and the fact
that he had signed Jefferson Davis's bail-bond
made the "crow" more palatable to the Southern
Democrats.   In the campaign Greeley's brilliant
speeches were listened to with great respect.   His
tour was a personal triumph; but the very voters
who hung eagerly on his speeches felt him to be too
impulsive and opinionated to be trusted with presidential powers.   They knew the worst which might
be expected of Grant; they could not guess the ruin
which Greeley's dynamic powers might bring on
the country if he used them unwisely.   In the end
many of the original leaders of the Liberal movement supported Grant as the lesser of two evils.
The Liberal defection from the Republican ranks
was more than offset by the refusal of Democrats
to vote for Greeley, and Grant was triumphantly
reëlected.

The Liberal Republican party was undoubtedly
weakened by the unfortunate selection of its candidate, but it scarcely could have been victorious
with another candidate.   The movement was distinctly one of leaders rather than of the masses, and
the things for which it stood most specifically —
the removal of political disabilities in the South and
civil service reform — awakened little enthusiasm

among the farmers of the West. These farmers on the other hand were beginning to be very much interested in a number of economic reforms which would vitally affect their welfare, such as the reduction and readjustment of the burden of taxation, the control of corporations in the interests of the people, the reduction and regulation of the cost of transporation, and an increase in the currency supply. Some of these propositions occasionally received recognition in Liberal speeches and platforms, but several of them were anathema to many of the Eastern leaders of that movement. Had these leaders been gifted with vision broad enough to enable them to appreciate the vital economic and social problems of the West, the Liberal Republican movement might perhaps have caught the ground swell of agrarian discontent, and the outcome might then have been the formation of an enduring national party of liberal tendencies broader and more progressive than the Liberal Republican party yet less likely to be swept into the vagaries of extreme radicalism than were the Anti-Monopoly and Greenback parties of after years. A number of western Liberals such as A. Scott Sloan in Wisconsin and Ignatius Donnelly in Minnesota championed the farmers' cause, it is true, and in

some States there was a fusion of party organizations; but men like Schurz and Trumbull held aloof
from these radical movements, while Easterners
like Godkin of the *Nation* met them with ridicule
and invective.

The period from 1870 to 1873 has been characterized as one of rampant prosperity, and such it was
for the commercial, the manufacturing, and especially the speculative interests of the country.   For
the farmers, however, it was a period of bitter depression.   The years immediately following the
close of the Civil War had seen a tremendous expansion of production, particularly of the staple
crops.   The demobilization of the armies, the closing of war industries, increased immigration, the
homestead law, the introduction of improved
machinery, and the rapid advance of the railroads
had all combined to drive the agricultural frontier
westward by leaps and bounds until it had almost
reached the limit of successful cultivation under
conditions which then prevailed.   As crop acreage
and production increased, prices went down in ac-
cordance with the law of supply and demand, and
farmers all over the country found it difficult to
make a living.

In the West and South — the great agricultural

districts of the country — the farmers commonly bought their supplies and implements on credit or mortgaged their crops in advance; and their profits at best were so slight that one bad season might put them thereafter entirely in the power of their creditors and force them to sell their crops on their creditors' terms. Many farms were heavily mortgaged, too, at rates of interest that ate up the farmers' profits. During and after the Civil War the fluctuation of the currency and the high tariff worked especial hardship on the farmers as producers of staples which must be sold abroad in competition with European products and as consumers of manufactured articles which must be bought at home at prices made arbitrarily high by the protective tariff. In earlier times, farmers thus harassed would have struck their tents and moved farther west, taking up desirable land on the frontier and starting out in a fresh field of opportunity. It was still possible for farmers to go west, and many did so but only to find that the opportunity for economic independence on the edge of settlement had largely disappeared. The era of the self-sufficing pioneer was drawing to a close, and the farmer on the frontier, forced by natural conditions over which he had no control to engage in the production of staples, was fully as dependent on the market and on transportation facilities as was his competitor in the East.

In the fall of 1873 came the greatest panic in the history of the nation, and a period of financial depression began which lasted throughout the decade, restricting industry, commerce, and even immigration. On the farmers the blow fell with special severity. At the very time when they found it most difficult to realize profit on their sales of produce, creditors who had hitherto carried their debts from year to year became insistent for payment. When mortgages fell due, it was well-nigh impossible to renew them; and many a farmer saw years of labor go for nothing in a heart-breaking foreclosure sale. It was difficult to get even short-term loans, running from seed-time to harvest. This important function of lending money to pay for labor and thus secure a larger crop, which has only recently been assumed by the Government in its establishment of farm loan banks, had been performed by private capitalists who asked usurious rates of interest. The farmers' protests against these rates had been loud; and now, when they found themselves unable to get loans at any rate whatever, their complaints naturally increased.

Looking around for one cause to which to attribute all their misfortunes, they pitched upon the corporations or monopolies, as they chose to call them, and especially upon the railroads.

At first the farmers had looked upon the coming of the railroads as an unmixed blessing. The railroad had meant the opening up of new territory, the establishment of channels of transportation by which they could send their crops to market. Without the railroad, the farmer who did not live near a navigable stream must remain a backwoodsman; he must make his own farm or his immediate community a self-sufficing unit; he must get from his own land bread and meat and clothing for his family; he must be stock-raiser, grain-grower, farrier, tinker, soap-maker, tanner, chandler — Jack-of-all-trades and master of none. With the railroad he gained access to markets and the opportunity to specialize in one kind of farming; he could now sell his produce and buy in exchange many of the articles he had previously made for himself at the expense of much time and labor. Many farmers and farming communities bought railroad bonds in the endeavor to increase transportation facilities; all were heartily in sympathy with the policy of the Government in granting to corporations land along the route of the railways which they were to construct.

By 1873, however, the Government had actually given to the railroads about thirty-five million acres, and was pledged to give to the Pacific roads alone about one hundred and forty-five million acres more. Land was now not so plentiful as it had been in 1850, when this policy had been inaugurated, and the farmers were naturally aggrieved that the railroads should own so much desirable land and should either hold it for speculative purposes or demand for it prices much higher than the Government had asked for land adjacent to it and no less valuable. Moreover, when railroads were merged and reorganized or passed into the hands of receivers the shares held by farmers were frequently wiped out or were greatly decreased in value. Often railroad stock had been "watered" to such an extent that high freight charges were necessary in order to permit the payment of dividends. Thus the farmer might find himself without his railroad stock, with a mortgage on his land which he had incurred in order to buy the stock, with an increased burden of taxation because his township had also been gullible enough to buy stock, and with a railroad whose excessive rates allowed him but a narrow margin of profit on his produce.

When the farmers sought political remedies for their economic ills, they discovered that, as a class, they had little representation or influence either in Congress or in the state legislatures. Before the Civil War the Southern planter had represented agricultural interests in Congress fairly well; after the War the dominance of Northern interests left the Western farmer without his traditional ally in the South. Political power was concentrated in the East and in the urban sections of the West. Members of Congress were increasingly likely to be from the manufacturing classes or from the legal profession, which sympathized with these classes rather than with the agriculturists. Only about seven per cent of the members of Congress were farmers; yet in 1870 forty-seven per cent of the population was engaged in agriculture. The only remedy for the farmers was to organize themselves as a class in order to promote their common welfare.

CHAPTER III

WITH these real or fancied grievances crying for redress, the farmers soon turned to the Grange as the weapon ready at hand to combat the forces which they believed were conspiring to crush them. In 1872 began the real spread of the order. Where the Grange had previously reckoned in terms of hundreds of new lodges, it now began to speak of thousands. State Granges were established in States where the year before the organization had obtained but a precarious foothold; pioneer local Granges invaded regions which hitherto had been impenetrable. Although the only States which were thoroughly organized were Iowa, Minnesota, South Carolina, and Mississippi, the rapid spread of the order into other States and its intensive growth in regions so far apart gave promise of its ultimate development into a national movement.

This development was, to be sure, not without

opposition.   When the Grangers began to speak of their function in terms of business and political co-operation, the forces against which they were uniting took alarm.   The commission men and local merchants of the South were especially apprehensive and, it is said, sometimes foreclosed the mortgages of planters who were so independent as to join the order.   But here, as elsewhere, persecution defeated its own end; the opposition of their enemies convinced the farmers of the merits of the Grange.

In the East, several circumstances retarded the movement.   In the first place, the Eastern farmer had for some time felt the Western farmer to be his serious rival.   The Westerner had larger acreage and larger yields from his virgin soil than the Easterner from his smaller tracts of well-nigh exhausted land.   What crops the latter did produce he must sell in competition with the Western crops, and he was not eager to lower freight charges for his competitor.   A second deterrent to the growth of the order in the East was the organization of two Granges among the commission men and the grain dealers of Boston and New York, under the ægis of that clause of the constitution which declared any person interested in agriculture to be eligible to membership in the order.   Though the storm of protest which arose all over the country against this betrayal to the enemy resulted in the revoking of the charters for these Granges, the Eastern farmer did not soon forget the incident.

The year 1873 is important in the annals of the Grange because it marks the retirement of the "founders" from power. In January of that year, at the sixth session of the National Grange, the temporary organization of government clerks was replaced by a permanent corporation, officered by farmers. Kelley was reëlected Secretary; Dudley W. Adams of Iowa was made Master; and William Saunders, erstwhile Master of the National Grange, D. Wyatt Aiken of South Carolina, and E. R. Shankland of Iowa were elected to the executive committee. The substitution of alert and eager workers, already experienced in organizing Granges, for the dead wood of the Washington bureaucrats gave the order a fresh impetus to growth. From the spring of 1873 to the following spring the number of granges more than quadrupled, and the increase again centered mainly in the Middle West.

By the end of 1873 the Grange had penetrated all but four States — Connecticut, Rhode Island, Delaware, and Nevada — and there were thirty-two state Granges in existence. The movement was now well defined and national in scope, so that the seventh annual session of the National Grange, which took place in St. Louis in February, 1874, attracted much interest and comment.   Thirty-three men and twelve women attended the meetings, representing thirty-two state and territorial Granges and about half a million members.   Their most important act was the adoption of the "Declaration of Purposes of the National Grange," subscribed to then and now as the platform of the Patrons and copied with minor modifications by many later agricultural organizations in the United States.   The general purpose of the Patrons was "to labor for the good of our Order, our Country, and Mankind."   This altruistic ideal was to find practical application in efforts to enhance the comfort and attractions of homes, to maintain the laws, to advance agricultural and industrial education, to diversify crops, to systematize farm work, to establish coöperative buying and selling, to suppress personal, local, sectional, and national prejudices, and to discountenance "the credit system, the fashion system, and every other system tending to prodigality and bankruptcy."   As to business, the Patrons declared themselves enemies not of capital but of the tyranny of monopolies, not of railroads but of their high freight tariffs and monopoly of transportation. In politics, too, they maintained a rather nice balance: the Grange was not to be a political or party organization, but its members were to perform their political duties as individual citizens.

It could hardly be expected that the program of the Grange would satisfy all farmers. For the agricultural discontent, as for any other dissatisfaction, numerous panaceas were proposed, the advocates of each of which scorned all the others and insisted on their particular remedy. Some farmers objected to the Grange because it was a secret organization; others, because it was nonpartisan. For some the organization was too conservative; for others, too radical. Yet all these objectors felt the need of some sort of organization among the farmers, very much as the trade-unionist and the socialist, though widely divergent in program, agree that the workers must unite in order to better their condition. Hence during these years of activity on the part of the Grange many other agricultural societies were formed, differing from the Patrons of Husbandry in specific program rather than in general purpose.

The most important of these societies were the

farmers' clubs, at first more or less independent of each other but later banded together in state associations. The most striking differences of these clubs from the Granges were their lack of secrecy and their avowed political purposes. Their establishment marks the definite entrance of the farmers as a class into politics. During the years 1872 to 1875 the independent farmers' organizations multiplied much as the Granges did and for the same reasons. The Middle West again was the scene of their greatest power. In Illinois this movement began even before the Grange appeared in the State, and its growth during the early seventies paralleled that of the secret order. In other States also, notably in Kansas, there sprang up at this time agricultural clubs of political complexion, and where they existed in considerable numbers they generally took the lead in the political activities of the farmers' movement. Where the Grange had the field practically to itself, as in Iowa and Minnesota, the restriction in the constitution of the order as to political or partisan activity was evaded by the simple expedient of holding meetings "outside the gate," at which platforms were adopted, candidates nominated, and plans made for county, district, and state conventions.

In some cases the farmers hoped, by a show of strength, to achieve the desired results through one or both of the old parties, but they soon decided that they could enter politics effectively only by way of a third party. The professional politicians were not inclined to espouse new and radical issues which might lead to the disruption of party lines. The outcome, therefore, was the establishment of new parties in eleven of the Western States during 1873 and 1874. Known variously as Independent, Reform, Anti-Monopoly, or Farmers' parties, these organizations were all parts of the same general movement, and their platforms were quite similar. The paramount demands were: first, the subjection of corporations, and especially of railroad corporations, to the control of the State; and second, reform and economy in government. After the new parties were well under way, the Democrats in most of the States, being in a hopeless minority, made common cause with them in the hope of thus compassing the defeat of their hereditary rivals, the old-line Republicans. In Missouri, however, where the Democracy had been restored to power by the Liberal-Republican movement, the new party received the support of the Republicans.

Illinois, where the farmers were first thoroughly

organized into clubs and Granges, was naturally the
first State in which they took effective political action.   The agitation for railroad regulation, which
began in Illinois in the sixties, had caused the new
state constitution of 1870 to include mandatory
provisions directing the legislature to pass laws to
prevent extortion and unjust discrimination in railway charges.   One of the acts passed by the Legislature of 1871 in an attempt to carry out these instructions was declared unconstitutional by the
state supreme court in January, 1873.   This was
the spark to the tinder.   In the following April the
farmers flocked to a convention at the state capital
and so impressed the legislators that they passed
more stringent and effective laws for the regulation
of railroads.   But the politicians had a still greater
surprise in store for them.   In the elections of
judges in June, the farmers retired from office the
judge who had declared their railroad law unconstitutional and elected their own candidates for the
two vacancies in the supreme court and for many
of the vacancies in the circuit courts.

Now began a vigorous campaign for the election
of farmers' candidates in the county elections in the
fall.   So many political meetings were held on Independence Day in 1873 that it was referred to as

IGNATIUS DONNELLY

Drawing from a photograph.

the "Farmers' Fourth of July." This had always been the greatest day of the farmer's year, for it meant opportunity for social and intellectual enjoyment in the picnics and celebrations which brought neighbors together in hilarious good-fellowship. In 1873, however, the gatherings took on unwonted seriousness. The accustomed spread-eagle oratory gave place to impassioned denunciation of corporations and to the solemn reading of a *Farmers' Declaration of Independence*. "When, in the course of human events," this document begins in words familiar to every schoolboy orator, "it becomes necessary for a class of the people, suffering from long continued systems of oppression and abuse, to rouse themselves from an apathetic indifference to their own interests, which has become habitual . . . a decent respect for the opinions of mankind requires that they should declare the causes that impel them to a course so necessary to their own protection." Then comes a statement of "self-evident truths," a catalogue of the sins of the railroads, a denunciation of railroads and Congress for not having redressed these wrongs, and finally the conclusion:

We, therefore, the producers of the state in our several counties assembled . . . do solemnly declare

3

that we will use all lawful and peaceable means to free ourselves from the tyranny of monopoly, and that we will never cease our efforts for reform until every department of our Government gives token that the reign of licentious extravagance is over, and something of the purity, honesty, and frugality with which our fathers inaugurated it, has taken its place.

That to this end we hereby declare ourselves absolutely free and independent of all past political connections, and that we will give our suffrage only to such men for office, as we have good reason to believe will use their best endeavors to the promotion of these ends; and for the support of this declaration, with a firm reliance on divine Providence, we mutually pledge to each other our lives, our fortunes, and our sacred honor.

This fall campaign of 1873 in Illinois broke up old party lines in remarkable fashion. In some counties the Republicans and in other counties the Democrats either openly joined the "Reformers" or refrained from making separate nominations. Of the sixty-six counties which the new party contested, it was victorious in fifty-three. This first election resulted in the best showing which the Reformers made in Illinois. In state elections, the new party was less successful; the farmers who voted for their neighbors running on an Anti-Monopoly ticket for lesser offices hesitated to vote for strangers for state office.

Other Middle Western States at this time also felt the uneasy stirring of radical political thought and saw the birth of third parties, short-lived, most of them, but throughout their brief existence crying loudly and persistently for reforms of all description. The tariff, the civil service system, and the currency, all came in for their share of criticism and of suggestions for revision, but the dominant note was a strident demand for railroad regulation. Heirs of the Liberal Republicans and precursors of the Greenbackers and Populists, these independent parties were as voices crying in the wilderness, preparing the way for national parties of reform. The notable achievement of the independent parties in the domain of legislation was the enactment of laws to regulate railroads in five States of the upper Mississippi Valley.[1] When these laws were passed, the parties had done their work. By 1876 they had disappeared or, in a few instances, had merged with the Greenbackers. Their temporary successes had demonstrated, however, to both farmers and professional politicians that if once solidarity could be obtained among the agricultural class, that class would become the controlling element in the politics of the Middle Western States. It is not

[1] See Chapter IV.

surprising, therefore, that wave after wave of reform swept over the West in the succeeding decades.

The independent parties of the middle seventies were distinctly spontaneous uprisings of the people and especially of the farmers, rather than movements instigated by politicians for personal ends or by professional reformers. This circumstance was a source both of strength and weakness. As the movements began to develop unexpected power, politicians often attempted to take control but, where they succeeded, the movement was checked by the farmers' distrust of these self-appointed leaders. On the other hand, the new parties suffered from the lack of skillful and experienced leaders. The men who managed their campaigns and headed their tickets were usually well-to-do farmers drafted from the ranks, with no more political experience than perhaps a term or two in the state legislature. Such were Willard C. Flagg, president of the Illinois State Farmers' Association, Jacob G. Vale, candidate for governor in Iowa, and William R. Taylor, the Granger governor of Wisconsin.

Taylor is typical of the picturesque and forceful figures which frontier life so often developed. He was born in Connecticut, of parents recently emigrated from Scotland. Three weeks after his birth his mother died, and six years later his father, a sea captain, was drowned. The orphan boy, brought up by strangers in Jefferson County, New York, experienced the hardships of frontier life and developed that passion for knowledge which so frequently is found in those to whom education is denied. When he was sixteen, he had enough of the rudiments to take charge of a country school, and by teaching in the winter and working in the summer he earned enough to enter Union College. He was unable to complete the course, however, and turned to teaching in Ohio, where he restored to decent order a school notorious for bullying its luckless teachers. But teaching was not to be his career; indeed, Taylor's versatility for a time threatened to make him the proverbial Jack-of-all-trades: he was employed successively in a grist mill, a saw mill, and an iron foundry; he dabbled in the study of medicine; and finally, in the year which saw Wisconsin admitted to the Union, he bought a farm in that State. Ownership of property steadied his interests and at the same time afforded an adequate outlet for his energies. He soon made his farm a model for the neighborhood and managed it so efficiently that he had time to interest himself in farmers' organizations and to hold positions of trust in his township and county.

By 1873 Taylor had acquired considerable local political experience and had even held a seat in the state senate. As president of the State Agricultural Society, he was quite naturally chosen to head the ticket of the new Liberal Reform party. The brewing interests of the State, angered at a drastic temperance law enacted by the preceding legislature, swung their support to Taylor. Thus reënforced, he won the election. As governor he made vigorous and tireless attempts to enforce the Granger railroad laws, and on one occasion he scandalized the conventional citizens of the State by celebrating a favorable court decision in one of the Granger cases with a salvo of artillery from the capitol.

Yet in spite of this prominence, Taylor, after his defeat for reëlection in 1875, retired to his farm and to obscurity. His vivid personality was not again to assert itself in public affairs. It is difficult to account for the fact that so few of the leaders during the Granger period played prominent parts in later phases of the agrarian crusade. The rank and file of the successive parties must have been much the same, but each wave of the movement swept new leaders to the surface.

The one outstanding exception among the leaders of the Anti-Monopolists was Ignatius Donnelly of Minnesota — "the sage of Nininger" — who remained a captain of the radical cohorts in every agrarian movement until his death in 1901. A red-headed aggressive Irishman, with a magnetic personality and a remarkable intellect, Donnelly went to Minnesota from Pennsylvania in 1856 and speculated in town sites on a large scale. When he was left stranded by the panic of 1857, acting upon his own principle that "to hide one's light under a bushel is to extinguish it," he entered the political arena. In Pennsylvania Donnelly had been a Democrat, but his genuine sympathy for the oppressed made him an opponent of slavery and consequently a Republican. In 1857 and 1858 he ran for the state senate in Minnesota on the Republican ticket in a hopelessly Democratic county. In 1859 he was nominated for lieutenant governor on the ticket headed by Alexander Ramsey; and his caustic wit, his keenness in debate, and his eloquence made him a valuable asset in the battle-royal between Republicans and Democrats for the possession of Minnesota. As lieutenant governor, Donnelly early showed his sympathy with the farmers by championing laws which lowered the

legal rate of interest and which made more humane
the process of foreclosure on mortgages. The out-
break of the Civil War gave him an opportunity to
demonstrate his executive ability as acting governor during Ramsey's frequent trips to Washington.
In this capacity he issued the first proclamation for
the raising of Minnesota troops in response to the
call of President Lincoln. Elected to Congress in
1862, he served three terms and usually supported
progressive legislation.

Donnelly's growing popularity and his ambition
for promotion to the Senate soon became a matter of alarm to the friends of Senator Ramsey,
who controlled the Republican party in the State.
They determined to prevent Donnelly's renomi-
nation in 1868 and selected William D. Washburn
of Minneapolis to make the race against him. In
the spring of this year Donnelly engaged in a controversy with Representative E. B. Washburn of
Illinois, a brother of W. D. Washburn, in the
course of which the Illinois congressman published
a letter in a St. Paul paper attacking Donnelly's
personal character. Believing this to be part of the
campaign against him, the choleric Minnesotan re-
plied in the house with a remarkable rhetorical
display which greatly entertained the members but

did not increase their respect for him. His opponents at home made effective use of this affair, and the outcome of the contest was a divided convention, the nomination of two Republicans, each claiming to be the regular candidate of the party, and the ultimate election of a Democrat.

Donnelly was soon ready to break with the old guard of the Republican party in national as well as in state politics. In 1870 he ran for Congress as an independent Republican on a low tariff platform but was defeated in spite of the fact that he received the endorsement of the Democratic convention. Two years later he joined the Liberal Republicans in supporting Greeley against Grant. When the farmers' Granges began to spring up like mushrooms in 1873, Donnelly was quick to see the political possibilities of the movement. He conducted an extensive correspondence with farmers, editors, and politicians of radical tendencies all over the State and played a leading part in the organization of the Anti-Monopoly party. He was elected to the state senate in 1873, and in the following year he started a newspaper, the *Anti-Monopolist*, to serve as the organ of the movement.

Although Donnelly was technically still a farmer, he was quite content to leave the management of his

farm to his capable wife, while he made politics his
profession, with literature and lecturing as avoca-
tions. His frequent and brilliant lectures no less
than his voluminous writings[1] attest his amazing
industry. Democrat, Republican, Liberal-Republican, and Anti-Monopolist; speculator, lawyer,
farmer, lecturer, stump-speaker, editor, and author;
preacher of morals and practicer of shrewd political
evasions; and always a radical — he was for many
years a force to be reckoned with in the politics of
his State and of the nation.

[1] *The Great Cryptogram*, for instance, devotes a thousand pages to
proving a Bacon cipher in the plays of Shakespeare!

CHAPTER IV

THOUGH the society of the Patrons of Husbandry was avowedly non-political in character, there is ample justification for the use of the term "Granger" in connection with the radical railroad legislation enacted in the Northwestern States during the seventies. The fact that the Grange did not take direct political action is immaterial: certainly the order made political action on the part of the farmers possible by establishing among them a feeling of mutual confidence and trust whereby they could organize to work harmoniously for their common cause. Before the advent of the Patrons of Husbandry the farmers were so isolated from each other that coöperation was impossible. It is hard for us to imagine, familiar as we are with the rural free delivery of mail, with the country telephone line, with the automobile, how completely the average farmer of 1865 was cut off from communication

43

with the outside world. His dissociation from any but his nearest neighbors made him unsocial, narrow-minded, bigoted, and suspicious. He believed that every man's hand was against him, and he was therefore often led to turn his hand against every man. Not until he was convinced that he might at least trust the Grangers did he lay aside his suspicions and join with other farmers in the attempt to obtain what they considered just railroad legislation.

Certain it is, moreover, that the Grangers made use of the popular hostility to the railroads in securing membership for the order. "Coöperation" and "Down with Monopoly" were two of the slogans most commonly used by the Grange between 1870 and 1875 and were in large part responsible for its great expansion. Widely circulated reprints of articles exposing graft and corruption made excellent fuel for the flames of agitation.

How much of the farmers' bitterness against the railroads was justified it is difficult to determine. Some of it was undoubtedly due to prejudice, to the hostility of the "producer" for the "nonproducer," and to the suspicion which the Western farmer felt for the Eastern magnate. But much of the suspicion was not without foundation. In some cases manipulation of railway stock had absolutely cheated farmers and agricultural towns and counties out of their investments. It is a well-known fact that the corporations were not averse to creating among legislators a disposition to favor their interests. Passes were commonly given by the railroads to all public officials, from the local supervisors to the judges of the Supreme Court, and opportunities were offered to legislators to buy stock far below the market price. In such subtle ways the railroads insinuated themselves into favor among the makers and interpreters of law. Then, too, the farmers felt that the railway companies made rates unnecessarily high and frequently practised unfair discrimination against certain sections and individuals. When the Iowa farmer was obliged to burn corn for fuel, because at fifteen cents a bushel it was cheaper than coal, though at the same time it was selling for a dollar in the East, he felt that there was something wrong, and quite naturally accused the railroads of extortion.

The fundamental issue involved in Illinois, Minnesota, Iowa, and Wisconsin, where the battle was begun and fought to a finish, was whether or not a State had power to regulate the tariffs of railway companies incorporated under its laws.

Railway companies, many jurists argued, were private concerns transacting business according to the laws of the State and no more to be controlled in making rates than dry goods companies in fixing the price of spools of thread; rates, like the price of merchandise, were determined by the volume of trade and the amount of competition, and for a State to interfere with them was nothing less than tyranny. On the other hand, those who advocated regulation argued that railroads, though private corporations, were from the nature of their business public servants and, as such, should be subject to state regulation and control.

Some States, foreseeing difficulties which might arise later from the doctrine that a charter is a contract, as set forth by the United States Supreme Court in the famous Dartmouth College case,[1] had quite early in their history attempted to safeguard their right to legislate concerning corporations. A clause had been inserted in the state constitution of Wisconsin which declared that all laws creating corporations might at any time be altered or repealed by the legislatures. The constitution of Minnesota asserted specifically that the railroads,

---

[1] See *John Marshall and the Constitution*, by Edward S. Corwin (in *The Chronicles of America*), p. 154 ff.

as common carriers enjoying right of way, were bound to carry freight on equal and reasonable terms. When the Legislature of Iowa turned over to the railroad companies lands granted by the Federal Government, it did so with the reservation that the companies should be subject to the rules and regulations of the General Assembly. Thus these States were fortified not only by arguments from general governmental theory but also by written articles, more or less specifically phrased, on which they relied to establish their right to control the railroads.

The first gun in this fight for railroad regulation was fired in Illinois. As early as 1869, after several years of agitation, the legislature passed an act declaring that railroads should be limited to "just, reasonable, and uniform rates," but, as no provision was made for determining what such rates were, the act was a mere encumbrance on the statute books. In the new state constitution of 1870, however, the framers, influenced by a growing demand on the part of the farmers which manifested itself in a Producers' Convention, inserted a section directing the legislature to "pass laws to correct abuses and to prevent unjust discrimination and extortion in the rates of freight and passenger tariffs on the different railroads in this State." The legislature at its next session appears to have made an honest attempt to obey these instructions. One act established maximum passenger fares varying from two and one-half to five and one-half cents a mile for the different classes into which the roads were divided. Another provided, in effect, that freight charges should be based entirely upon distance traversed and prohibited any increases over rates in 1870. This amounted to an attempt to force all rates to the level of the lowest competitive rates of that year. Finally, a third act established a board of railroad and warehouse commissioners charged with the enforcement of these and other laws and with the collection of information.

The railroad companies, denying the right of the State to regulate their business, flatly refused to obey the laws; and the state supreme court declared the act regulating freight rates unconstitutional on the ground that it attempted to prevent not only unjust discrimination but any discrimination at all. The legislature then passed the Act of 1873, which avoided the constitutional pitfall by providing that discriminatory rates should be considered as *prima facie* but not absolute evidence of unjust discrimination. The railroads were thus permitted to adduce evidence to show that the discrimination was justified, but the act expressly stated that the existence of competition at some points and its nonexistence at others should not be deemed a sufficient justification of discrimination. In order to prevent the roads from raising all rates to the level of the highest instead of lowering them to the level of the lowest, the commissioners were directed to establish a schedule of maximum rates; and the charging of rates higher than these by any company after January 15, 1874, was to be considered *prima facie* evidence of extortion. Other provisions increased the penalties for violations and strengthened the enforcing powers of the commission in other ways. This act was roundly denounced at the time, especially in the East, as an attempt at confiscation, and the railroad companies refused to obey it for several years; but ultimately it stood the test of the courts and became the permanent basis of railroad regulation in Illinois and the model for the solution of this problem in many other States.

The first Granger law of Minnesota, enacted in 1871, established fixed schedules for both passengers and freight, while another act of the same year

provided for a railroad commissioner. In this
instance also the companies denied the validity of
the law, and when the state supreme court upheld it
in 1873, they appealed to the Supreme Court of the
United States. In the meantime there was no
way of enforcing the law, and the antagonism toward the roads fostered by the Grange and the
Anti-Monopoly party became more and more intense. In 1874 the legislature replaced the Act of
1871 with one modeled on the Illinois law of 1873;
but it soon discovered that no workable set of uniform rates could be made for the State because of
the wide variation of conditions in the different
sections. Rates and fares which would be just to
the companies in the frontier regions of the State
would be extortionate in the thickly populated
areas. This difficulty could have been avoided by
giving the commission power to establish varying
schedules for different sections of the same road;
but the anti-railroad sentiment was beginning to
die down, and the Legislature of 1875, instead of
trying to improve the law, abandoned the attempt
at state regulation.

The Granger laws of Iowa and Wisconsin, both
enacted in 1874, attempted to establish maximum rates by direct legislative action, although

commissions were also created to collect information and assist in enforcing the laws. The Iowa law was very carefully drawn and appears to have been observed, in form at least, by most of the companies while it remained in force. In 1878, however, a systematic campaign on the part of the railroad forces resulted in the repeal of the act. In Wisconsin, a majority of the members of the Senate favored the railroads and, fearing to show their hands, attempted to defeat the proposed legislation by substituting the extremely radical Potter Bill for the moderate measure adopted by the Assembly. The senators found themselves hoist with their own petard, however, for the lower house, made up largely of Grangers, accepted this bill rather than let the matter of railroad legislation go by default. The rates fixed by the Potter Law for many commodities were certainly unreasonably low, although the assertion of a railroad official that the enforcement of the law would cut off twenty-five per cent of the gross earnings of the companies was a decided exaggeration. Relying upon the advice of such eminent Eastern lawyers as William M. Evarts, Charles O'Conor, E. Rockwood Hoar, and Benjamin R. Curtis that the law was invalid, the roads refused to obey it until it was

upheld by the state supreme court late in 1874.
They then began a campaign for its repeal. Though
they obtained only some modification in 1875, they
succeeded completely in 1876.

The contest between the railroads and the farmers was intense while it lasted. The farmers had
votes; the railroads had money; and the legislators
were sometimes between the devil and the deep sea
in the fear of offending one side or the other. The
farmers' methods of campaign were simple. Often
questionnaires were distributed to all candidates for
office, and only those who went on record as favoring railroad restriction were endorsed by the farmers' clubs and committees. An agricultural convention, sometimes even a meeting of the state
Grange, would be held at the capital of the State
while the legislature was in session, and it was a
bold legislator who, in the presence of his farmer
constituents, would vote against the measures they
approved. When the railroads in Illinois refused
to lower their passenger rates to conform to the law,
adventurous farmers often attempted to "ride for
legal fares," giving the trainmen the alternative
of accepting the low fares or throwing the hardy
passengers from the train.

The methods of the railroads in dealing with the

legislators were more subtle. Whether or not the numerous charges of bribery were true, railroad favors were undoubtedly distributed among well disposed legislators. In Iowa passes were not given to the senators who voted against the railroads, and those sent to the men who voted in the railroads' interest were accompanied by notes announcing that free passes were no longer to be given generally but only to the friends of the railroads. At the session of the Iowa Legislature in 1872, four lawyers who posed as farmers and Grange members were well known as lobbyists for the railroads. The senate paid its respects to these men at the close of its session by adopting the following resolution:

WHEREAS, There have been constantly in attendance on the Senate and House of this General Assembly, from the commencement of the session to the present time, four gentlemen professing to represent the great agricultural interest of the State of Iowa, known as the Grange; and —

WHEREAS, These gentlemen appear entirely destitute of any visible means of support; therefore be it —

RESOLVED, By the Senate, the House concurring, that the janitors permit aforesaid gentlemen to gather up all the waste paper, old newspapers, &c., from under the desks of the members, and they be allowed one postage stamp each, *The American Agriculturist*, *What Greeley Knows about Farming*, and that they be permitted to take with them to their homes, if they have any, all the rejected railroad tariff bills, Beardsley's speech on female suffrage, Claussen's reply, Kasson's speech on barnacles, Blakeley's dog bill, Teale's liquor bill, and be given a pass over the Des Moines Valley Railroad, with the earnest hope that they will never return to Des Moines.

Once the Granger laws were enacted, the railroads either fought the laws in court or obeyed them in such a way as to make them appear most obnoxious to the people, or else they employed both tactics. The lawsuits, which began as soon as the laws had been passed, dragged on, in appeal after appeal, until finally they were settled in the Supreme Court of the United States. These suits were not so numerous as might be expected, because in most of the States they had to be brought on the initiative of the injured shipper, and many shippers feared to incur the animosity of the railroad. A farmer was afraid that, if he angered the railroad, misfortunes would befall him: his grain might be delivered to the wrong elevators or left to stand and spoil in damp freight cars; there might be no cars available for grain just when his shipment was ready; and machinery destined for him might be delayed at a time when lack of it would mean the loss of his crops. The railroads for their part whenever they found an opportunity to make the new laws appear obnoxious in the eyes of the people, were not slow to seize it.   That section of the Illinois law of 1873 which prohibited unjust discrimination went into effect in July, but the maximum freight rates were not fixed until January of 1874. As a result of this situation, the railroads in July made all their freight rates uniform, according to the law, but accomplished this uniformity by raising the low rates instead of lowering the high.   In Minnesota, similarly, the St. Paul and Pacific road, in its zeal to establish uniform passenger rates, raised the fare between St. Paul and Minneapolis from three to five cents a mile, in order to make it conform to the rates elsewhere in the State.   The St. Paul and Sioux City road declared that the Granger law made its operation unprofitable, and it so reduced its train service that the people petitioned the commission to restore the former rate. In Wisconsin, when the state supreme court affirmed the constitutionality of the radical Potter law, the railroads retaliated in some cases by carrying out their threat to give the public "Potter cars, Potter rails, and Potter time."   As a result the public soon demanded the repeal of the law.

In all the States but Illinois the Granger laws were

repealed before they had been given a fair trial.
The commissions remained in existence, however,
although with merely advisory functions; and they
sometimes did good service in the arbitration of dis-
putes between shippers and railroads.   Interest in
the railroad problem died down for the time, but
every one of the Granger States subsequently enacted for the regulation of railroad rates statutes which,
although more scientific than the laws of the seventies, are the same in principle. The Granger laws
thus paved the way not only for future and more enduring legislation in these States but also for similar
legislation in most of the other States of the Union
and even for the national regulation of railroads
through the Interstate Commerce Commission.

The Supreme Court of the United States was the
theater for the final stage of this conflict between
the railroads and the farmers.   In October, 1876,
decisions were handed down together in eight cases
which had been appealed from federal circuit and
state courts in Illinois, Wisconsin, Iowa, and Minnesota, and which involved the validity of the
Granger laws.   The fundamental issue was the
same in all these cases — the right of a State to
regulate a business that is public in nature though
privately owned and managed.

The first of the "Granger cases," as they were termed by Justice Field in a dissenting opinion, was not a railroad case primarily but grew out of warehouse legislation which the farmers of Illinois secured in 1871. This act established maximum charges for grain storage and required all warehousemen to publish their rates for each year during the first week in January and to refrain from increasing these rates during the year and from discriminating between customers. In an endeavor to enforce this law the railroad and warehouse commission brought suit against Munn and Scott, a warehouse firm in Chicago, for failure to take out the license required by the act. The suit, known as Munn *vs.* Illinois, finally came to the United States Supreme Court and was decided in favor of the State, two of the justices dissenting.[1] The opinion of the court in this case, delivered by Chief Justice Waite, laid down the principles which were followed in the railroad cases. The attorneys for the warehousemen had argued that the act in question, by assuming to limit charges, amounted to a deprivation of property without due process of law and was thus repugnant to the Fourteenth Amendment to the Constitution of the United States.

[1] *94 United States Reports*, 113.

But the court declared that it had long been customary both in England and America to regulate by law any business in which the public has an interest, such as ferries, common carriers, bakers, or millers, and that the warehouse business in question was undoubtedly clothed with such a public interest. Further, it was asserted that this right to regulate implied the right to fix maximum charges, and that what those charges should be was a legislative and not a judicial question.

In deciding the railroad cases the courts applied the same general principles, the public nature of the railroad business having already been established by a decision in 1872.[1] Another point was involved, however, because of the contention of the attorneys for the companies that the railway charters were contracts and that the enforcement of the laws would amount to an impairment of contracts, which was forbidden by the Constitution. The court admitted that the charters were contracts but denied that state regulation could be considered an impairment of contracts unless the terms of the charter were specific. Moreover, it was pointed out that contracts must be interpreted in the light of rights reserved to the State in its constitution

[1] Olcott *vs.* The Supervisors, 16 Wallace, 678.

and in the light of its general laws of incorporation under which the charters were granted.

These court decisions established principles which even now are of vital concern to business and politics. From that time to this no one has denied the right of States to fix maximum charges for any business which is public in its nature or which has been clothed with a public interest; nor has the inclusion of the railroad and warehouse businesses in that class been questioned. The opinion, however, that this right of the States is unlimited, and therefore not subject to judicial review, has been practically reversed. In 1890 the Supreme Court declared a Minnesota law invalid because it denied a judicial hearing as to the reasonableness of rates[1]; and the courts now assume it to be their right and duty to determine whether or not rates fixed by legislation are so low as to amount to a deprivation of property without due process of law. In spite of this later limitation upon the power of the States, the Granger decisions have furnished the legal basis for state regulation of railroads down to the present day. They are the most significant achievements of the anti-monopoly movement of the seventies.

[1] 134 *United States Reports*, 418.

CHAPTER V

THE COLLAPSE OF THE GRANGER MOVEMENT

THE first phase of the agrarian crusade, which centered around and took its distinctive name from the Grange, reached its highwater mark in 1874. Early in the next year the tide began to ebb. The number of Granges decreased rapidly during the remainder of the decade, and of over twenty thousand in 1874 only about four thousand were alive in 1880.

Several causes contributed to this sudden decline. Any organization which grows so rapidly is prone to decay with equal rapidity; the slower growths are better rooted and are more likely to reach fruition. So with the Grange. Many farmers had joined the order, attracted by its novelty and vogue; others joined the organization in the hope that it would prove a panacea for all the ills that agriculture is heir to and then left it in disgust when they found its success neither immediate nor universal.

Its methods of organization, too, while admirably adapted to arousing enthusiasm and to securing new chapters quickly, did not make for stability and permanence. The Grange deputy, as the organizer was termed, did not do enough of what the salesman calls "follow-up work." He went into a town, persuaded an influential farmer to go about with him in a house-to-house canvass, talked to the other farmers of the vicinity, stirred them up to interest and excitement, organized a Grange, and then left the town. If he happened to choose the right material, the chapter became an active and flourishing organization; if he did not choose wisely, it might drag along in a perfunctory existence or even lapse entirely. Then, too, the deputy's ignorance of local conditions sometimes led him to open the door to the farmers' enemies. There can be little doubt that insidious harm was worked through the admission into the Grange of men who were farmers only incidentally and whose "interest in agriculture" was limited to making profits from the farmer rather than from the farm. As D. Wyatt Aiken, deputy for the Grange in the Southern States and later member of the executive committee of the National Grange, shrewdly commented, "Everybody wanted to join the Grange then; lawyers, to get clients; doctors, to get customers; Shylocks, to get their pound of flesh; and sharpers, to catch the babes in the woods.''

Not only the members who managed thus to insinuate themselves into the order but also the legitimate members proved hard to control. With that hostility to concentrated authority which so often and so lamentably manifests itself in a democratic body, the rank and file looked with suspicion upon the few men who constituted the National Grange. The average farmer was interested mainly in local issues, conditions, and problems, and looked upon the National Grange not as a means of helping him in local affairs, but as a combination of monopolists who had taken out a patent on the local grange and forced him to pay a royalty in order to enjoy its privileges. The demand for reduction in the power of the National Grange led to frequent attempts to revise the constitution in the direction of decentralization; and the revisions were such as merely to impair the power of the National Grange without satisfying the discontented members.

Of all the causes of the rapid collapse of the Granger movement, the unfortunate experience which the farmers had in their attempts at business coöperation was probably chief. Their hatred of the middleman and of the manufacturer was almost as intense as their hostility to the railroad magnate; quite naturally, therefore, the farmers attempted to use their new organizations as a means of eliminating the one and controlling the other. As in the parallel case of the railroads, the farmers' animosity, though it was probably greater than the provocation warranted, was not without grounds.

The middlemen — the commission merchants to whom the farmer sold his produce and the retail dealers from whom he bought his supplies — did undoubtedly make use of their opportunities to drive hard bargains. The commission merchant had such facilities for storage and such knowledge of market conditions that he frequently could take advantage of market fluctuations to increase his profits. The farmer who sold his produce at a low price and then saw it disposed of as a much higher figure was naturally enraged, but he could devise no adequate remedy. Attempts to regulate market conditions by creating an artificial shortage seldom met with success. The slogan "Hold your hogs" was more effective as a catchword than as an economic weapon. The retail dealers, no less than the commission men, seemed to the farmer to be unjust in their dealings with him. In the small agricultural communities there was practically no competition. Even where there were several merchants in one town these could, and frequently did, combine to fix prices which the farmer had no alternative but to pay. What irked the farmer most in connection with these "extortions" was that the middleman seemed to be a non-producer, a parasite who lived by draining the agricultural classes of the wealth which they produced. Even those farmers who recognized the middleman as a necessity had little conception of the intricacy and value of his service.

Against the manufacturer, too, the farmer had his grievances. He felt that the system of patent rights for farm machinery resulted in unfair prices — for was not this same machinery shipped to Europe and there sold for less than the retail price in the United States? Any one could see that the manufacturer must have been making more than reasonable profit on domestic sales. Moreover, there were at this time many abuses of patent rights. Patents about to expire were often extended through political influence or renewed by means of slight changes which were claimed to be improvements. A more serious defect in the patent system was that new patents were not thoroughly investigated, so that occasionally one was issued on an article which had long been in common use. That a man should take out a patent for the manufacture of a sliding gate which farmers had for years crudely constructed for themselves and should then collect royalty from those who were using the gates they had made, naturally enough aroused the wrath of his victims.

It was but natural, then, that the Granges should be drawn into all sorts of schemes to divert into the pockets of their members the streams of wealth which had previously flowed to the greedy middlemen. The members of the National Grange, thinking that these early schemes for coöperation were premature, did not at first take them up and standardize them but left them entirely in the hands of local, county, and state Granges. These thereupon proceeded to "gang their ain gait" through the unfamiliar paths of business operations and too frequently brought up in a quagmire. "This purchasing business," said Kelley in 1867, "commenced with buying jackasses; the prospects are that many will be *sold*." But the Grangers went on with their plans for business coöperation with ardor undampened by such forebodings. Sometimes

5

a local Grange would make a bargain with a certain dealer of the vicinity, whereby members were allowed special rates if they bought with cash and traded only with that dealer. More often the local grange would establish an agency, with either a paid or a voluntary agent who would forward the orders of the members in large lots to the manufacturers or wholesalers and would thus be able to purchase supplies for cash at terms considerably lower than the retail prices. Frequently, realizing that they could get still more advantageous terms for larger orders, the Granges established a county agency which took over the work of several local agents. Sometimes the Patrons even embarked upon the more ambitious enterprise of coöperative stores.

The most common type of coöperative store was that in which the capital was provided by a stock company of Grange members and which sold goods to Patrons at very low prices. The profits, when there were any, were divided among the stockholders in proportion to the amount of stock they held, just as in any stock company. This type of store was rarely successful for any length of time. The low prices at which it sold goods were likely to involve it in competition with other merchants.

Frequently these men would combine to lower their prices and, by a process familiar in the history of business competition, "freeze out" the coöperative store, after which they might restore their prices to the old levels. The farmers seldom had sufficient spirit to buy at the Grange store if they found better bargains elsewhere; so the store was assured of its clientèle only so long as it sold at the lowest possible prices. Farmers' agencies for the disposal of produce met with greater success. Coöperative creameries and elevators in several States are said to have saved Grange members thousands of dollars. Sometimes the state Grange, instead of setting up in the business of selling produce, chose certain firms as Grange agents and advised Patrons to sell through these firms. Where the choice was wisely made, this system seems to have saved the farmers about as much money without involving them in the risks of business.

By 1876 the members of the National Grange had begun to study the problem of coöperation in retailing goods and had come to the conclusion that the so-called "Rochdale plan," a system worked out by an English association, was the most practicable for the coöperative store. The National Grange therefore recommended this type of organization. The stock of these stores was sold only to Patrons, at five dollars a share and in limited amounts; thus the stores were owned by a large number of stockholders, all of whom had equal voice in the management of the company. The stores sold goods at ordinary rates, and then at the end of the year, after paying a small dividend on the stock, divided their profits among the purchasers, according to the amounts purchased. This plan eliminated the violent competition which occurred when a store attempted to sell goods at cost, and at the same time saved the purchaser quite as much. Unfortunately the Rochdale plan found little favor among farmers in the Middle West because of their unfortunate experience with other coöperative ventures. In the East and South, however, it was adopted more generally and met with sufficient success to testify to the wisdom of the National Grange in recommending it.

In its attitude toward manufacturing, the National Grange was less sane. Not content with the elimination of the middlemen, the farmers were determined to control the manufacture of their implements. With the small manufacturer they managed to deal fairly well, for they could usually find some one who would supply the Grange with implements at less than the retail price. In Iowa, where the state Grange early established an agency for coöperative buying, the agent managed to persuade a manufacturer of plows to give a discount to Grangers. As a result, this manufacturer's plows are reported to have left the factory with the paint scarcely dry, while his competitors, who had refused to make special terms, had difficulty in disposing of their stock. But the manufacturers of harvesters persistently refused to sell at wholesale rates. The Iowa Grange thereupon determined to do its own manufacturing and succeeded in buying a patent for a harvester which it could make and sell for about half what other harvesters cost. In 1874 some 250 of these machines were manufactured, and the prospects looked bright.

Deceived by the apparent success of grange manufacturing in Iowa, officers of the order at once planned to embark in manufacturing on a large scale. The National Grange was rich in funds at this time; it had within a year received well over $250,000 in dispensation fees from seventeen thousand new Granges. Angered at what was felt to be the tyranny of monopoly, the officers of the National Grange decided to use this capital in manufacturing agricultural implements which were to be sold to Patrons at very low prices. They went about the country buying patents for all sorts of farm implements, but not always making sure of the worth of the machinery or the validity of the patents. In Kansas, Iowa, Missouri, Wisconsin, Illinois, Indiana, and Kentucky, they planned factories to make harvesters, plows, wagons, sewing-machines, threshing-machines, and all sorts of farm implements. Then came the crash. The Iowa harvester factory failed in 1875 and bankrupted the state Grange. Other failures followed; suits for patent infringements were brought against some of the factories; local Granges disbanded for fear they might be held responsible for the debts incurred; and in the Northwest, where the activity had been the greatest, the order almost disappeared.

Although the Grange had a mushroom growth, it nevertheless exerted a real and enduring influence upon farmers both as individuals and as members of a class. Even the experiments in coöperation, disastrous though they were in the end, were not without useful results. While they lasted they undoubtedly effected a considerable saving for the farmers. As Grange agents or as stockholders in coöperative stores or Grange factories, many farmers gained valuable business experience which helped to prevent them from being victimized thereafter. The farmers learned, moreover, the wisdom of working through the accepted channels of business. Those who had scoffed at the Rochdale plan of coöperation, in the homely belief that any scheme made in America must necessarily be better than an English importation, came to see that self-confidence and independence must be tempered by willingness to learn from the experience of others. Most important of all, these experiments in business taught the farmers that the middlemen and manufacturers performed services essential to the agriculturalist and that the production and distribution of manufactured articles and the distribution of crops are far more complex affairs than the farmers had imagined and perhaps worthy of more compensation than they had been accustomed to think just. On their side, the manufacturers and dealers learned that the farmers were not entirely helpless and that to gain their goodwill by fair prices was on the whole wiser than to force them into competition. Thus these ventures resulted in the development of a new tolerance and a new respect between the two traditionally antagonistic classes.

The social and intellectual stimulus which the

farmers received from the movement was probably
even more important than any direct political or
economic results. It is difficult for the present
generation to form any conception of the dreari-
ness and dullness of farm life half a century ago.
Especially in the West, where farms were large, opportunities for social intercourse were few, and
weeks might pass without the farmer seeing any
but his nearest neighbors.   For his wife existence
was even more drear. She went to the market
town less often than he and the routine of her life
on the farm kept her close to the farmhouse and
prevented visits even to her neighbors' dwellings.
The difficulty of getting domestic servants made
the work of the farmer's wife extremely laborious;
and at that time there were none of the modern
conveniences which lighten work such as power
churns, cream separators, and washing-machines.
Even more than the husband, the wife was likely to
degenerate into a drudge without the hope — and
eventually without the desire — of anything better.
The church formed, to be sure, a means of social
intercourse; but according to prevailing religious
notions the churchyard was not the place nor the
Sabbath the time for that healthy but unrestrained
hilarity which is essential to the well-being of man.

Into lives thus circumscribed the Grange came as a liberalizing and uplifting influence. Its admission of women into the order on the same terms as men made it a real community servant and gave both women and men a new sense of the dignity of woman. More important perhaps than any change in theories concerning womankind, it afforded an opportunity for men and women to work and play together, apparently much to the satisfaction and enjoyment of both sexes. Not only in Grange meetings, which came at least once a month and often more frequently, but also in Grange picnics and festivals the farmers and their wives and children came together for joyous human intercourse. Such frequent meetings were bound to work a change of heart. Much of man's self-respect arises from the esteem of others, and the desire to keep that esteem is certainly a powerful agent in social welfare. It was reported that in many communities the advent of the Grange created a marked improvement in the dress and manners of the members. Crabbed men came out of their shells and grew genial; disheartened women became cheerful; repressed children delighted in the chance to play with other boys and girls of their own age.

The ritual of the Grange, inculcating lessons of

orderliness, industry, thrift, and temperance, expressed the members' ideals in more dignified and pleasing language than they themselves could have invented. The songs of the Grange gave an opportunity for the exercise of the musical sense of people not too critical of literary quality, when with "spontaneous trills on every tongue," as one of the songs has it, the members varied the ritual with music.

One of the virtues especially enjoined on Grange members was charity. Ceres, Pomona, and Flora, offices of the Grange to be filled only by women, were made to represent Faith, Hope, and Charity, respectively; and in the ceremony of dedicating the Grange hall these three stood always beside the altar while the chaplain read the thirteenth chapter of First Corinthians. Not only in theory but in practice did the order proclaim its devotion to charitable work. It was not uncommon for members of a local Grange to foregather and harvest the crops for a sick brother or help rebuild a house destroyed by fire or tornado. In times of drought or plague both state and national Granges were generous in donations for the sufferers; in 1874, when the Mississippi River overflowed its banks in its lower reaches, money and supplies were sent to the farmers of Louisiana and Alabama; again in the same year relief was sent to those Patrons who suffered from the grasshopper plague west of the Mississippi; and in 1876 money was sent to South Carolina to aid sufferers from a prolonged drought in that State. These charitable deeds, endearing giver and receiver to each other, resulted in a better understanding and a greater tolerance between people of different parts of the country.

The meetings of the local Granges were forums in which the members trained themselves in public speaking and parliamentary practice. Programs were arranged, sometimes with the help of suggestions from officers of the state Grange; and the discussion of a wide variety of topics, mostly economic and usually concerned especially with the interests of the farmer, could not help being stimulating, even if conclusions were sometimes reached which were at variance with orthodox political economy. The Grange was responsible, too, for a great increase in the number and circulation of agricultural journals. Many of these papers were recognized as official organs of the order and, by publishing news of the Granges and discussing the political and economic phases of the farmers' movement, they built up an extensive circulation. Rural postmasters everywhere reported a great increase in their mails after the establishment of a Grange in the vicinity.   One said that after the advent of the order there were thirty newspapers taken at his office where previously there had been but one. Papers for which members or local Granges subscribed were read, passed from hand to hand, and thoroughly discussed.   This is good evidence that farmers were forming the habit of reading.   All the Granger laws might have been repealed; all the schemes for coöperation might have come to naught; all the moral and religious teachings of the Grange might have been left to the church; but if the Granger movement had created nothing else than this desire to read, it would have been worth while.   For after the farmer began to read, he was no longer like deadwood floating in the backwaters of the current; he became more like a propelled vessel in midstream — sometimes, to be sure, driven into turbulent waters, sometimes tossed about by conflicting currents, but at least making progress.

CHAPTER VI

WHATEVER may have been the causes of the collapse of the Granger movement in 1875 and 1876, returning prosperity for the Western farmer was certainly not one of them, for the general agricultural depression showed no signs of lifting until nearly the end of the decade. During the Granger period the farmer attempted to increase his narrow margin of profit or to turn a deficit into a profit by decreasing the cost of transportation and eliminating the middleman. Failing in this attempt, he decided that the remedy for the situation was to be found in increasing the prices for his products and checking the appreciation of his debts by increasing the amount of money in circulation.

This demand for currency inflation was by no means new when it was taken up by the Western farmers. It had played a prominent part in American history from colonial days, especially in

77

periods of depression and in the less prosperous sections of the ever advancing frontier. During the Civil War, inflation was actually accomplished through the issue of over $400,000,000 in legal-tender notes known as "greenbacks." No definite time for the redemption of these notes was specified, and they quickly declined in value as compared with gold. At the close of the war a paper dollar was worth only about half its face value in gold. An attempt was made to raise the relative value of the greenbacks and to prepare for the resumption of specie payments by retiring the paper money from circulation as rapidly as possible. This policy meant, of course, a contraction of the volume of currency and consequently met with immediate opposition. In February, 1868, Congress prohibited the further retirement of greenbacks and left to the discretion of the Secretary of the Treasury the reissue of the $44,000,000 which had been retired. Only small amounts were reissued, however, until after the panic of 1873; and when Congress attempted, in April, 1874, to force a permanent increase of the currency to $400,000,000, President Grant vetoed the bill.

Closely related to the currency problem was that of the medium to be used in the payment of the principal of bonds issued during the Civil War. When the bonds were sold, it was generally understood that they would be redeemed in gold or its equivalent. Some of the issues, however, were covered by no specific declaration to that effect, and a considerable sentiment arose in favor of redeeming them with currency, or lawful money, as it was called.

These questions were not party issues at first, and there was no clear-cut division upon them between the two old parties throughout the period. The alinement was by class and section rather than by party; and inflationists and advocates of the redemption of the bonds in currency were to be found not only among the rank and file but also among the leaders of both parties. The failure of either the Democrats or the Republicans to take a decided stand on these questions resulted, as so often before, in the development of third parties which made them the main planks in the new platform.

The first attempts at organized political activity in behalf of greenbackism came not from the farmers of the West but from the laboring men of the East, whose growing class consciousness resulted in the organization of the National Labor Union in 1868. Accompanying, if not resulting from the

Government's policy of contraction, came a fall of prices and widespread unemployment. It is not strange, therefore, that this body at once declared itself in favor of inflation. The plan proposed was what was known as the "American System of Finance": money was to be issued only by the Government and in the form of legal-tender paper redeemable only with bonds bearing a low rate of interest, these bonds in turn to be convertible into greenbacks at the option of the holder. The National Labor Union recommended the nomination of workingmen's candidates for offices and made arrangements for the organization of a National Labor party. This convened in Columbus in February, 1872, adopted a Greenback platform, and nominated David Davis of Illinois as its candidate for the presidency. After the nomination of Horace Greeley by the Liberal Republicans, Davis declined this nomination, and the executive committee of his party then decided that it was too late to name another candidate.

This early period of inflation propaganda has been described as "the social reform period, or the wage-earners' period of greenbackism, as distinguished from the inflationist, or farmers' period that followed." The primary objects of the labor reformers were, it appears, to lower the rate of interest on money and to reduce taxation by the transformation of the war debt into interconvertible bonds. The farmers, on the other hand, were interested primarily in the expansion of the currency in the hope that this would result in higher prices for their products. It was not until the panic of 1873 had intensified the agricultural depression and the Granger movement had failed to relieve the situation that the farmers of the West took hold of greenbackism and made it a major political issue.

The independent parties of the Granger period, as a rule, were not in favor of inflation. Their platforms in some cases demanded a speedy return to specie payment. In 1873 Ignatius Donnelly, in a pamphlet entitled *Facts for the Granges*, declared: "There is too much paper money. The currency is *diluted — watered — weakened*. . . . We have no interest in an inflated money market. . . . As we have to sell our wheat at the world's price, it is our interest that everything we buy should be at the world's price. Specie payments would practically add eighteen cents to the price of every bushel of wheat we have to sell!" In Indiana and Illinois, however, the independent parties were captured by the Greenbackers, and

6

the Indiana party issued the call for the conference at Indianapolis in November, 1874, which led to the organization of the National Greenback party.

This conference was attended by representatives from seven States and included several who had been prominent in the Labor Reform movement. "The political Moses of the 'New Party,'" according to the Chicago *Tribune*, was James Buchanan of Indianapolis, a lawyer "with an ability and shrewdness that compel respect, however much his theories may be ridiculed and abused." He was also the editor of the *Sun*, a weekly paper which supported the farmers' movement. The platform committee of the conference reported in favor of "a new political organization of the people, by the people, and for the people, to restrain the aggressions of combined capital upon the rights and interests of the masses, to reduce taxation, correct abuses, and to purify all departments of the Government." The most important issue before the people was declared to be "the proper solution of the money question," meaning thereby the issue of greenbacks interconvertible with bonds. A national convention of the party was called to meet at Cleveland on March 11, 1875.

The Cleveland convention, attended by representatives of twelve States, completed the organization of the Independent party, as it was officially named, and made arrangements for the nominating convention. This was held at Indianapolis on May 17, 1876, with 240 delegates representing eighteen States. Ignatius Donnelly, who had apparently changed his mind on the currency question since 1873, was the temporary president. The platform contained the usual endorsement of a circulating medium composed of legal-tender notes interconvertible with bonds but gave first place to a demand for "the immediate and unconditional repeal of the specie-resumption act." This measure, passed by Congress in January, 1875, had fixed January 1, 1879, as the date when the Government would redeem greenbacks at their face value in coin. Although the act made provision for the permanent retirement of only a part of the greenbacks from circulation, the new party denounced it as a "suicidal and destructive policy of contraction." Another plank in the platform, and one of special interest in view of the later free silver agitation, was a protest against the sale of bonds for the purpose of purchasing silver to be substituted for the fractional currency of war times.

This measure, it was asserted, "although well calculated to enrich owners of silver mines . . . will still further oppress, in taxation, an already overburdened people."

There was a strong movement in the convention for the nomination of David Davis for the presidency, but this seems to have met with opposition from Eastern delegates who remembered his desertion of the National Labor Reform party in 1872. Peter Cooper of New York was finally selected as the candidate.   He was a philanthropist rather than a politician and was now eighty-five years old. Having made a large fortune as a pioneer in the manufacture of iron, he left his business cares to other members of his family and devoted himself to the education and elevation of the working classes.   His principal contribution to this cause was the endowment of the famous Cooper Union in New York, where several thousand persons, mostly mechanics, attended classes in a variety of technical and educational subjects and enjoyed the privileges of a free library and reading room. When notified of his nomination, Cooper at first expressed the hope that one or both of the old parties might adopt such currency planks as would make the new movement unnecessary.   Later he accepted unconditionally but took no active part in the campaign.

The Greenback movement at first made but slow progress in the various States. In Indiana and Illinois the existing independent organizations became component parts of the new party, although in Illinois, at least, quite a number of the former leaders returned to the old parties. In the other Western States, however, the third parties of the Granger period had gone to pieces or had been absorbed by means of fusion, and new organizations had to be created. In Indiana the Independent party developed sufficient strength to scare the Republican leaders and to cause one of them to write to Hayes: "A bloody-shirt campaign, with money, and Indiana is safe; a financial campaign and no money and we are beaten."

The Independents do not appear to have made a very vigorous campaign in 1876. The coffers of the party were as empty as the pockets of the farmers who were soon to swell its ranks; and this made a campaign of the usual sort impossible. One big meeting was held in Chicago in August, with Samuel F. Cary, the nominee for Vice-President, as the principal attraction; and this was followed by a torchlight procession. A number of papers published by men who were active in the movement, such as Buchanan's *Indianapolis Star*, Noonan's *Industrial Age* of Chicago, and Donnelly's *Anti-Monopolist* of St. Paul, labored not without avail to spread the gospel among their readers. The most effective means of propaganda, however, was probably the Greenback Club. At a conference in Detroit in August, 1875, "the organization of Greenback Clubs in every State in the Union" was recommended, and the work was carried on under the leadership of Marcus M. Pomeroy. "Brick" Pomeroy was a journalist, whose sobriquet resulted from a series of *Brickdust Sketches* of prominent Wisconsin men which he published in one of his papers. As the editor of *Brick Pomeroy's Democrat*, a sensational paper published in New York, he had gained considerable notoriety. In 1875, after the failure of this enterprise he undertook to retrieve his broken fortunes by editing a Greenback paper in Chicago and by organizing Greenback clubs for which this paper served as an organ. Pomeroy also wrote and circulated a series of tracts with such alluring titles as *Hot Drops* and *Meat for Men*. Several thousand clubs were organized in the Northwest during the next few years, principally in the rural regions, and the secrecy of their proceedings aroused the fear that they were advocating communism. The members of the clubs and their leaders constituted, as a matter of fact, the more radical of the Greenbackers. They usually opposed fusion with the Democrats and often refused to follow the regular leaders of the party.

In the election the Greenback ticket polled only about eighty thousand votes, or less than one per cent of the total. In spite of the activity of former members of the Labor Reform party in the movement, Pennsylvania was the only Eastern State in which the new party made any considerable showing. In the West over 6000 votes were cast in each of the five States — Indiana, Illinois, Michigan, Iowa, and Kansas. The agrarian aspect of the movement was now uppermost, but the vote of 17,000 polled in Illinois, though the largest of the group, was less than a quarter of the votes cast by the state Independent Reform party in 1874 when railroad regulation had been the dominant issue. Clearly many farmers were not yet convinced of the necessity of a Greenback party. The only tangible achievement of the party in 1876 was the election of a few members of the Illinois Legislature who held the balance between the old parties and were instrumental in sending David Davis to the

United States Senate. This vote, it is interesting to note, kept Davis from serving on the electoral commission and thus probably prevented Tilden from becoming President.

But the Greenback movement was to find fresh impetus in 1877, a year of exceptional unrest and discontent throughout the Union. The agricultural depression was even greater than in preceding years, while the great railroad strikes were evidence of the distress of the workingmen. This situation was reflected in politics by the rapid growth of the Greenback party and the reappearance of labor parties with Greenback planks.[1]

In the following year the new party had an excellent opportunity to demonstrate its strength wherever it existed. In February, 1878, a conference was held at Toledo for the purpose of welding the various political organizations of workingmen

[1] In state elections from Massachusetts to Kansas the Greenback and labor candidates polled from 5 to 15 per cent of the total vote, and in most cases the Greenback vote would probably have been much greater had not one or the other, and in some cases both, of the old parties incorporated part of the Greenback demands in their platforms. In Wisconsin, for example, there was little difference between Democrats and Greenbackers on the currency question, and even the Republicans in their platform leaned toward inflation, although the candidates declared against it. No general elections were held in 1877 in some of the States where the Greenback sentiment was most pronounced.

and advocates of inflation into an effective weapon as a single united party.   This conference, which was attended by several hundred delegates from twenty-eight States, adopted "National" as the name of the party, but it was usually known from this time on as the Greenback Labor party.   The Toledo platform, as the resolutions adopted by this conference came to be designated, first denounced "the limiting of the legal-tender quality of greenbacks, the changing of currency-bonds into coin-bonds, the demonetization of the silver dollar, the excepting of bonds from taxation, the contraction of the circulating medium, the proposed forced resumption of specie payments, and the prodigal waste of the public lands."   The resolutions which followed demanded the suppression of bank notes and the issue of all money by the Government, such money to be full legal-tender at its stamped value and to be provided in sufficient quantity to insure the full employment of labor and to establish a rate of interest which would secure to labor its just reward.   Other planks called for the coinage of silver on the same basis as that of gold, reservation of the public lands for actual settlers, legislative reduction of the hours of labor, establishment of labor bureaus, abolition of the contract system of employing prison labor, and suppression of Chinese immigration. It is clear that in this platform the interests of labor received full consideration. Just before the conference adjourned it adopted two additional resolutions. One of these, adopted in response to a telegram from General B. F. Butler, denounced the silver bill just passed by Congress because it had been so modified as to limit the amount of silver to be coined. The other, which was offered by "Brick" Pomeroy, declared: "We will not affiliate in any degree with any of the old parties, but in all cases and localities will organize anew . . . and . . . vote only for men who entirely abandon old party lines and organizations." This attempt to forestall fusion was to be of no avail, as the sequel will show, but Pomeroy and his followers in the Greenback clubs adhered throughout to their declaration.

In the elections of 1878, the high-water mark of the movement, about a million votes were cast for Greenback candidates. Approximately two-thirds of the strength of the party was in the Middle West and one-third in the East. That the movement, even in the East, was largely agrarian, is indicated by the famous argument of Solon Chase, chairman of the party convention in Maine. "Inflate the currency, and you raise the price of my steers and at the same time pay the public debt." "Them steers" gave Chase a prominent place in politics for half a decade. The most important achievement of the movement at this time was the election to Congress of fifteen members who were classified as Nationals — six from the East, six from the Middle West, and three from the South. In most cases these men secured their election through fusion or through the failure of one of the old parties to make nominations.

Easily first among the Greenbackers elected to Congress in 1878 was General James B. Weaver of Iowa. When ten years of age, Weaver had been taken by his parents to Iowa from Ohio, his native State. In 1854, he graduated from a law school in Cincinnati, and for some years thereafter practiced his profession and edited a paper at Bloomfield in Davis County, Iowa. He enlisted in the army as a private in 1861, displayed great bravery at the battles of Donelson and Shiloh, and received rapid promotion to the rank of colonel. At the close of the war he received a commission as brigadier general by brevet. Weaver ran his first tilt in state politics in an unsuccessful attempt to obtain the Republican nomination for lieutenant governor in

1865.   Although an ardent advocate of prohibition and of state regulation of railroads, Weaver remained loyal to the Republican party during the Granger period and in 1875 was a formidable candidate for the gubernatorial nomination.   It is said that a majority of the delegates to the convention had been instructed in his favor, but the railroad and liquor interests succeeded in stampeding the convention to Samuel J. Kirkwood, the popular war governor.   In the following year Weaver took part in the organization of the Independent or Greenback party in Iowa and accepted a position on its state committee.   Though resentment at the treatment which he had received from the Republicans may have influenced him to break the old ties, he was doubtless sincerely convinced that the Republican party was beyond redemption and that the only hope for reform lay in the new party movement.

Weaver was gifted with remarkable talent as an orator.   His fine face and soldierly bearing, his rich sympathetic voice and vivid imagination, made him a favorite speaker at soldiers' reunions and in political campaigns.   Lacking the eccentricities of so many of his third party associates and never inclined to go to extremes in his radicalism, he was

one of the ablest and, from the standpoint of the
Republicans, the most dangerous of the Greenback
leaders.   In Congress Weaver won the respect of
his colleagues.   Always ready to promote what he
believed to be the interests of the common people
and especially of the farmers, he espoused the cause
of the Oklahoma "boomers," who were opposed by
a powerful lobby representing the interests of the
"cattle barons."   He declared that, in a choice
between bullocks and babies, he would stand for
babies, and he staged a successful filibuster at the
close of a session in order to force the consideration
of a bill for the opening of part of Oklahoma to
settlement.

The preliminaries of the campaign of 1880 were
vexed by dissension within the ranks of the Greenbackers.   In March the radical faction led by
Pomeroy held a convention in St. Louis which
claimed to speak for ten thousand Greenback clubs
and two million voters.   After Stephen D. Dil-
laye of New York had refused the presidential
nomination at the hands of this convention, it adjourned to meet in Chicago on the 9th of June —
the place and time already selected for the regular
convention of the National party.   One reason for
the attitude of this faction appears to have been

the fear of fusion with the Democrats.   The Chicago convention finally succeeded in absorbing these malcontents, as well as a group of socialist delegates and representatives of various labor organizations who asked to be admitted.   Dennis Kearney, the notorious sand-lot agitator of California was made chief sergeant at arms, and Susan B. Anthony was allowed to give a suffrage speech. The platform differed from earlier Greenback documents in that it contained no denunciation of the Resumption Act.   That was now a dead issue, for on January 1, 1879, resumption became an accomplished fact, and the paper currency was worth its face value in gold.   Apart from this the platform was much the same as that adopted at Toledo in 1878, with the addition of planks favoring women's suffrage, a graduated income tax, and congressional regulation of interstate commerce.   On the first ballot, General Weaver received a majority of the votes for presidential nominee; and B. J. Chambers of Texas was nominated for Vice-President.

General Weaver in his letter of acceptance declared it to be his intention "to visit the various sections of the Union and talk to the people."   This he did, covering the country from Arkansas to Maine and from Lake Michigan to the Gulf, speaking in Faneuil Hall at Boston and in the Cooper Union at New York, but spending the greater part of his time in the Southern States. He declared that he traveled twenty thousand miles, made fully one hundred speeches, shook the hands of thirty thousand people, and was heard by half a million. Weaver was the first presidential candidate to conduct a campaign of this sort, and the results were not commensurate with his efforts. The Greenback vote was only 308,578, about three per cent of the total. One explanation of the small vote would seem to be the usual disinclination of people to vote for a man who has no chance of election, however much they may approve of him and his principles, when they have the opportunity to make their votes count in deciding between two other candidates. Then, too, the sun of prosperity was beginning at last to dissipate the clouds of depression. The crops of corn, wheat, and oats raised in 1880 were the largest the country had ever known; and the price of corn for once failed to decline as production rose, so that the crop was worth half as much again as that of 1878. When the farmer had large crops to dispose of at remunerative prices, he lost interest in the inflation of the currency.

After 1880 the Greenback party rapidly disintegrated. There was no longer any hope of its becoming a major party, in the near future at least, and the more conservative leaders began to drift back into the old parties or to make plans for fusion with one of them in coming elections. But fusion could at best only defer the end. The congressional election of 1882 clearly demonstrated that the party was moribund. Ten of the Congressmen elected in 1880 had been classified as Nationals; of these only one was reëlected in 1882, and no new names appear in the list. It is probable, however, that a number of Congressmen classified as Democrats owed their election in part to fusion between the Democratic and Greenback parties.

The last appearance of the Greenbackers in national politics was in the presidential election of 1884. In May of that year a convention of "The Anti-Monopoly Organization of the United States," held in Chicago, adopted a platform voicing a demand for legislative control of corporations and monopolies in the interests of the people and nominated General Benjamin F. Butler for President. The convention of the Greenback or National party met in Indianapolis, and selected Butler as its candidate also. General Weaver presided over

JAMES B. WEAVER

Photograph.

the convention.   The platform contained the usual
demands of the party with the exception of the resolution for the "free and unlimited coinage of gold
and silver," which was rejected by a vote of 218 to
164.   It would appear that the majority of the
delegates preferred to rely upon legal-tender paper
to furnish the ample supply of money desired.
General Butler was at this time acting with the
Democrats in Massachusetts, and his first response
was noncommittal.   Although he subsequently accepted both nominations, he did not make an active campaign, and his total popular vote was only
175,370.   Butler's personal popularity and his labor affiliations brought increased votes in some of
the Eastern States and in Michigan, but in those
Western States where the party had been strong-
est in 1880 and where it had been distinctly a farmers' movement there was a great falling off in the
Greenback vote.

Though the forces of agrarian discontent at-
tained national political organization for the first
time in the Greenback party, its leaders were never
able to obtain the support of more than a minority
of the farmers.   The habit of voting the Republican or the Democratic ticket, firmly established
by the Civil War and by Reconstruction, was too

7

strong to be lightly broken; and many who favored inflation could not yet bring themselves to the point of supporting the Greenback party. On the other hand there were undoubtedly many farmers and others who felt that the old parties were hopelessly subservient to capitalistic interests, who were ready to join in radical movements for reform and for the advancement of the welfare of the industrial classes, but who were not convinced that the structure of permanent prosperity for farmer and workingman could be built on a foundation of fiat money. Although the platforms of the Greenbackers contained many demands which were soundly progressive, inflation was the paramount issue in them; and with this issue the party was unable to obtain the support of all the forces of discontent, radicalism, and reform which had been engendered by the economic and political conditions of the times. The Greenback movement was ephemeral. Failing to solve the problem of agricultural depression, it passed away as had the Granger movement before it; but the greater farmers' movement of which both were a part went on.

CHAPTER VII

THE PLIGHT OF THE FARMER

AN English observer of agricultural conditions in
1893 finds that agricultural unrest was not peculiar
to the United States in the last quarter of the nineteenth century, but existed in all the more advanced
countries of the world:

Almost everywhere, certainly in England, France,
Germany, Italy, Scandinavia, and the United States,
the agriculturists, formerly so instinctively conservative, are becoming fiercely discontented, declare they
gained less by civilization than the rest of the community, and are looking about for remedies of a drastic
nature. In England they are hoping for aid from
councils of all kinds; in France they have put on protective duties which have been increased in vain twice
over; in Germany they put on and relaxed similar
duties and are screaming for them again; in Scandinavia — Denmark more particularly — they limit the
aggregation of land; and in the United States they
create organizations like the Grangers, the Farmers'
Leagues, and the Populists.[1]

[1] *The Spectator*, vol. LXX, p. 247.

It is to general causes, indeed, that one must turn before trying to find the local circumstances which aggravated the unrest in the United States, or at least appeared to do so. The application of power — first steam, then electricity — to machinery had not only vastly increased the productivity of mankind but had stimulated invention to still wider activity and lengthened the distance between man and that gaunt specter of famine which had dogged his footsteps from the beginning. With a constantly growing supply of the things necessary for the maintenance of life, population increased tremendously: England, which a few centuries before had been overcrowded with fewer than four million people, was now more bountifully feeding and clothing forty millions. Perhaps, all in all, mankind was better off than it had ever been before; yet different groups maintained unequal progress. The tillers of the soil as a whole remained more nearly in their primitive condition than did the dwellers of the city. The farmer, it is true, produced a greater yield of crops, was surrounded by more comforts, and was able to enjoy greater leisure than his kind had ever done before. The scythe and cradle had been supplanted by the mower and reaper; horse harrows, cultivators, and rakes had transferred much of the physical exertion of farming to the draft animals. But, after all, the farmer owed less to steam and electricity than the craftsman and the artisan of the cities.

The American farmer, if he read the census reports, might learn that rural wealth had increased from nearly $4,000,000,000 in 1850 to not quite $16,000,000,000 in 1890; but he would also discover that in the same period urban wealth had advanced from a little over $3,000,000,000 to more than $49,000,000,000. Forty years before the capital of rural districts comprised more than half that of the whole country, now it formed only twenty-five per cent. The rural population had shown a steady proportionate decrease: when the first census was taken in 1790, the dwellers of the country numbered more than ten times those of the city; but at the end of the nineteenth century they formed only about one-third of the total. Of course the intelligent farmer might have observed that food for the consumption of all could be produced by the work of fewer hands, and vastly more bountifully as well, and so he might have explained the relative decline of rural population and wealth; but when the average farmer saw his sons and his neighbors' sons more and more inclined to seek work in town and leave the farm, he put two and two together and came to the conclusion that farming was in a perilous state. He heard the boy who had gone to the city boast that his hours were shorter, his toil less severe, and his return in money much greater than had been the case on the farm; and he knew that this was true. Perhaps the farmer did not realize that he had some compensations: greater security of position and a reasonable expectation that old age would find him enjoying some sort of home, untroubled by the worry which might attend the artisan or shopkeeper.

Whether or not the American farmer realized that the nineteenth century had seen a total change in the economic relations of the world, he did perceive clearly that something was wrong in his own case. The first and most impressive evidence of this was to be found in the prices he received for what he had to sell. From 1883 to 1889 inclusive the average price of wheat was seventy-three cents a bushel, of corn thirty-six cents, of oats twenty-eight cents. In 1890 crops were poor in most of the grain areas, while prosperous times continued to keep the consuming public of the manufacturing regions able to buy; consequently corn and oats nearly doubled in price, and wheat advanced 20 per cent.   Nevertheless, such was the shortage, except in the case of corn, that the total return was smaller than it had been for a year or two before. In 1891 bumper crops of wheat, corn, oats, rye, and barley drove the price down on all except wheat and rye, but not to the level of 1889. Despite a much smaller harvest in 1892 the decline continued, to the intense disgust of the farmers of Nebraska and Minnesota who failed to note that the entire production of wheat in the world was normal in that year, that considerable stores of the previous crop had been held over and that more than a third of the yield in the United States was sent forth to compete everywhere with the crops of Argentine, Russia, and the other grain producing countries. No wonder the average farmer of the Mississippi basin was ready to give ear to any one who could suggest a remedy for his ills.

Cotton, which averaged nearly eleven cents a pound for the decade ending in 1890, dropped to less than nine cents in 1891 and to less than eight in 1892. Cattle, hogs, sheep, horses, and mules brought more in the late than in the early eighties, yet these, too, showed a decline about 1890. The abnormal war-time price of wool which was more than one dollar a pound in October, 1864, dropped precipitately with peace, rose a little just before the panic of 1873, and then declined with almost no reaction until it reached thirty-three cents for the highest grade in 1892.

The "roaring eighties," with all their superficial appearance of prosperity, had apparently not brought equal cheer to all. And then came the "heart-breaking nineties." In February, 1893, the Philadelphia and Reading Railroad Company failed, a break in the stock market followed, and an old-fashioned panic seized the country in its grasp. A period of hitherto unparalleled speculative frenzy came thus to an end, and sober years followed in which the American people had ample opportunity to contemplate the evils arising from their economic debauch.

Prices of agricultural products continued their downward trend. Wheat touched bottom in 1894 with an average price of forty-nine cents; corn, two years later, reached twenty-one cents. All the other grains were likewise affected. Middling cotton which had sold at eight and a half cents a pound in 1893, dropped below seven cents the following year, recovered until it reached nearly eight cents in 1896, and was at its lowest in 1898 at just under six cents. Of all the marketable products of the farm, cattle, hay, and hogs alone maintained the price level of the decade prior to 1892. Average prices, moreover, do not fully indicate the small return which many farmers received. In December, 1891, for instance, the average value of a bushel of corn was about forty cents, but in Nebraska, on January 1, 1892, corn brought only twenty-six cents. When, a few years later, corn was worth, according to the statistics, just over twenty-one cents, it was literally cheaper to burn it in Kansas or Nebraska than to cart it to town, sell it, and buy coal with the money received; and this is just what hundreds of despairing farmers did. Even crop shortage did little to increase the price of the grain that was raised. When a drought seriously diminished the returns in Ohio, Indiana, and Michigan in 1895, the importation from States farther west prevented any rise in price.

Prices dropped, but the interest on mortgages remained the same. One hundred and seventy-four bushels of wheat would pay the interest at 8 per cent on a $2000 mortgage in 1888, when the price of wheat was higher than it had been for ten years and higher than it was to be again for a dozen years. In 1894 or 1895 when the price was hovering around fifty cents, it took 320 bushels to pay the same interest. Frequently the interest was higher than 8 per cent, and outrageous commissions on renewals increased the burden of the farmer. The result was one foreclosure after another. The mortgage shark was identified as the servant of the "Wall Street Octopus," and between them there was little hope for the farmer. In Kansas, according to a contemporary investigator,[1] "the whole western third of the State was settled by a boom in farm lands. Multitudes of settlers took claims without means of their own, expecting to pay for the land from the immediate profits of farming. Multitudes of them mortgaged the land for improvements, and multitudes more expended the proceeds of mortgages in living. When it was found that the proceeds of farming in that part of the State were very uncertain, at best, the mortgages became due. And in many instances those who had been nominally owners remained upon the farms as tenants after foreclosure. These are but the natural effects in reaction from a tremendous boom." In eastern Kansas, where settlement was older, the pressure of hard times was withstood with less difficulty. It was in western Kansas, by the way, that Populism had its strongest following; and, after the election

[1] G. T. Fairchild, *Pol. Sc. Q.*, vol. 11, p. 614.

of 1892, a movement to separate the State into two commonwealths received serious consideration.

Even more inexorable than the holder of the mortgage or his agent was the tax collector. It was easy to demonstrate that the farmer, with little or nothing but his land, his stock, and a meager outfit of implements and furniture, all readily to be seen and assessed, paid taxes higher in proportion to his ability to pay than did the business man or the corporation. Although his equity in the land he owned might be much less than its assessed value, he was not allowed to make any deduction for mortgages. The revenue of the Federal Government was raised wholly by indirect taxes levied principally upon articles of common consumption; and the farmer and other people of small means paid an undue share of the burden in the form of higher prices demanded for commodities.

Low prices for his produce, further depressed by the rapacity of the railroads and the other intermediaries between the producer and the consumer, mortgages with high interest rates, and an inequitable system of taxation formed the burden of the farmer's complaint during the last two decades of the nineteenth century. These grievances and all sorts of remedies proposed for them were discussed in farmers' gatherings, in agricultural weeklies, even in city dailies, and ultimately in legislative chambers. Investigations demonstrated that, even when reduced to a minimum, the legitimate grounds for complaint were extensive; and the resultant reports suggested a variety of remedies. Generally, however, popular sentiment swung around again to the tack it had taken in the late seventies: the real cure for all the evils was more money. Wall Street and the national banks could suck the blood from the western community because of their monopoly of the money supply. According to one irate editor, "Few people are aware of the boundless advantages that the national banks have under our present accursed system. They have usurped the credit of the people and are fattening a thousand-fold annually from the unlimited resources at their command." Another editor wrote:

We find the following printed card on our desk: "The last report of the Secretary of the Treasury shows the banks as loaning $1,970,022,687"! Four times the amount of money there is to loan. Four interests in every dollar! They are drawing from the people enough to run the National Government. How long will it take them to gather in all the money of the nation? This does not include the amounts loaned by state, private, and savings banks. Add to this the billions of dollars of other loans and think if it is any wonder times are hard. Will the American people never wake up to the fact that they are being pauperized? Four people are paying interest upon each dollar you have in your pocket — if you have any. Wake up! Wake up!

Whatever the ultimate effects of an inflated and consequently depreciated currency might be, the debtor class, to which a large portion of the Western farmers belonged, would obviously benefit immediately by the injection of large quantities of money into the circulating medium. The purchasing power of money would be lower; hence the farmer would receive more in dollars and cents and would be in a better position to pay his standing debts. Whether or not the rise in the prices of his products would be offset or more than offset by the increased prices which he would have to pay for the things he purchased would depend upon the relative rate at which different commodities adjusted themselves to the new scale of money value. In the end, of course, other things being equal, there would be a return of old conditions; but the farmers did not look so far ahead. Hence it was that less attention was paid to taxation, to railroad rates and discriminations, to elevator companies, to grain gamblers, or to corporations as such; and the main force of the agrarian movements from 1875 onward was exerted, first for an increased paper currency and then for free silver.

CHAPTER VIII

THE FARMERS' ALLIANCE

THE hope of welding the farmers into an organization which would enable them to present a united front to their enemies and to work together for the promotion of their interests — social, economic, and political — was too alluring to be allowed to die out with the decline of the Patrons of Husbandry. Farmers who had experienced the benefits of the Grange, even though they had deserted it in its hour of trial, were easily induced to join another organization embodying all its essential features but proposing to avoid its mistakes. The conditions which brought about the rapid spread of the Grange in the seventies still prevailed; and as soon as the reaction from the Granger movement was spent, orders of farmers began to appear in various places and to spread rapidly throughout the South and West. This second movement for agricultural organization differed from the first in that it sprang from the soil, as it were, and, like Topsy, "just growed" instead of being deliberately planned and put into operation by a group of founders.

A local farmers' club or alliance was organized in 1874 or 1875 in the frontier county of Lampasas, Texas, for mutual protection against horse thieves and land sharks and for coöperation in the rounding up of strayed stock and in the purchase of supplies. That it might accomplish its purposes more effectively, the club adopted a secret ritual of three degrees; and it is said that at first this contained a formula for catching horse thieves. Affiliated lodges were soon established in neighboring communities, and in 1878 a Grand State Alliance was organized. Some one connected with this movement must have been familiar with the Grange, for the *Declaration of Purposes* adopted by the State Alliance in 1880 is but a crude paraphrase of the declaration adopted by the earlier order at St. Louis in 1874. These promising beginnings were quickly wrecked by political dissension, particularly in connection with the Greenback movement, and the first State Alliance held its last meeting in 1879. In that year, however, a member of the order who removed to Poolville in Parker County, Texas, organized there a distinctly non-partisan alliance.

From this new center the movement spread more rapidly; a second Grand State Alliance was organized; and the order grew with such rapidity that by 1886 there were nearly three thousand local lodges in the State. The social aspect was prominent in the Alliance movement in Texas from the beginning. Women were admitted to full membership, and negroes were excluded. In 1882 the three degrees of the ritual were combined into one so that all members might be on the same footing.

The early minutes of the State Alliance indicate that the rounding up of estrays was the most important practical feature of the order at that time, but in a few years this was overshadowed by coöperation. Trade agreements were made with dealers, joint stock stores and Alliance cottonyards were established, and finally a state exchange was organized with a nominal capital of half a million dollars to handle the business of the members. All the difficulties which the Grange had encountered in its attempts at coöperation beset the Alliance ventures: dissension was spread by merchants and commission men fighting for their livelihood; mistakes were made by agents and directors; too much was attempted at once; and in a few years the house of cards tumbled to the ground.

8

While its business ventures were still promising, the Texas Alliance came near being wrecked once more on the shoals of politics. The state meeting in August, 1886, adopted an elaborate set of "Demands," which included higher taxation of lands held for speculative purposes, prohibition of alien land ownership, laws to "prevent the dealing in futures of all agricultural products," full taxation of railroad property, "the rapid extinguishment of the public debt of the United States, by operating the mints to their fullest capacity in coining silver and gold, and the tendering of the same without discrimination to the public creditors," the issue of legal tender notes on a per capita basis and their substitution for bank notes, a national bureau of labor statistics, an interstate commerce law, and the abolition of the contract system of employing convicts. Provision was made for a committee of three to press these demands upon Congress and the State Legislature. At the close of the meeting, some of the members, fearing that the adoption of this report would lead to an attempt to establish a new political party, held another meeting and organized a rival State Alliance.

Considerable confusion prevailed for a few months; the president and vice-president of the regular State Alliance resigned, and the whole order seemed on the verge of disruption.   At this point there appeared on the stage the man who was destined not only to save the Alliance in Texas but also to take the lead in making it a national organization — C. W. Macune, the chairman of the executive committee.   Assuming the position of acting president, Macune called a special session of the State Alliance to meet in January, 1887.   At this meeting the constitution was amended to include a declaration that it was the purpose of the order "to labor for the education of the agricultural classes in the science of economical government, in a strictly nonpartisan spirit"; and attention was then directed to a plan for "the organization of the cotton belt of America."   The first step in this direction was taken in the same month when the Texas Alliance joined with the Farmers' Union of Louisiana and formed the National Farmers' Alliance and Coöperative Union of America. [1]

Macune, who was elected president of the

[1] The Farmers' Union was the outgrowth of an open farmers' club organized in Lincoln Parish, Louisiana, in 1880.   In 1885 this was transformed into a secret society with a ritual modeled after that of the Grange and with a constitution adapted from the constitution used by the Texas alliances.   Before the year was over the order spread into the adjoining parishes and a state union was established.

national body, at once sent organizers into most of the Southern States; and local alliances, followed rapidly by state organization, appeared in State after State. When the next meeting was held in October, 1887, delegates were present from nine Southern States.[1] The "Demands" adopted at this meeting were very like those which had split the Texas Alliance in the preceding year, with the addition of sections calling for the reduction of the tariff to a revenue basis, a graduated income tax, promotion of industrial and agricultural education, restriction of immigration, and popular election of United States senators.

As the Alliance spread into Arkansas and some of the adjoining States, it encountered another farmers' association of a very similar character and purpose. The Agricultural Wheel, as it was known, originated in a local club in Prairie County, Arkansas, in 1882, and soon expanded into a state-wide organization. After amalgamating with another agricultural order, known as the Brothers of Freedom, the Wheel began to roll into the adjoining States. In 1886 delegates from Tennessee and

[1] By December, 1888, it was claimed that there were 10,000 alliances in 16 States with a total membership of about 400,000. It was evident that the organization of the farmers of the cotton belt was rapidly being consummated.

Kentucky attended the meeting of the Arkansas State Wheel and took part in the organization of the National Agricultural Wheel.[1]   When the National Wheel held its first annual meeting in November, 1887, eight state organizations had been established, all in the Southwest, with a total membership of half a million.

With two great orders of farmers expanding in much the same territory and having practically identical objects, the desirability of union was obvious.   The subject was discussed at meetings of both bodies, and committees of conference were appointed.   Both organizations finally convened in December, 1888, at Meridian, Mississippi, and appointed a joint committee to work out the details of amalgamation.   The outcome was a new constitution, which was accepted by each body acting separately and was finally ratified by the state organizations.   The combined order was to be known as the Farmers' and Laborers' Union of America.

While this development had been going on in the South, another movement, somewhat different in character and quite independent in origin, had been

[1] Some difficulty was occasioned at this meeting by the question of admitting negroes to the order, but this was finally settled by making provision for separate lodges for colored members.

launched by the farmers of the Northwest. The founder of the National Farmers' Alliance, or the Northwestern Alliance, as it was called to distinguish it from the Southern organization, was Milton George, editor of the *Western Rural* of Chicago, who had been instrumental in organizing a local alliance in Cook County. This Alliance began issuing charters to other locals, and in October, 1880, at the close of a convention in Chicago, attended by "five hundred, representing alliances, granges, farmers' clubs, etc.," a national organization was formed. The constitution adopted at this time declared the object of the order to be "to unite the farmers of the United States for their protection against class legislation, and the encroachments of concentrated capital and the tyranny of monopoly; . . . to oppose, in our respective political parties, the election of any candidate to office, state or national, who is not thoroughly in sympathy with the farmers' interests; to demand that the existing political parties shall nominate farmers, or those who are in sympathy with them, for all offices within the gift of the people, and to do everything in a legitimate manner that may serve to benefit the producer." The specific measures for which the promoters of the Northwestern Alliance intended to work were set forth in a platform adopted at the second annual meeting in Chicago, October 5, 1881, which demanded: equal taxation of all property, including deduction of the amount of mortgages from assessments of mortgaged property; "a just income tax"; reduction of salaries of officials and their election instead of appointment, so far as practicable; regulation of interstate commerce; reform of the patent laws; and prevention of the adulteration of food. "The combination and consolidation of railroad capital . . . in the maintenance of an oppressive and tyrannical transportation system" was particularly denounced, and the farmers of the country were called upon to organize "for systematic and persistent action" for "the emancipation of the people from this terrible oppression."

The Northwestern Alliance did not attempt coöperation in business so extensively as did its Southern contemporaries, but a number of Alliance grain elevators were established in Minnesota and Dakota, coöperative creameries flourished in Illinois, and many of the alliances appointed agents to handle produce and purchase supplies for the members. It was in the field of politics, however, that the activity of the order was most notable. The methods by which the farmers of the Northwest attempted to use their organizations for political ends are well illustrated by the resolutions adopted at the annual meeting of the Minnesota State Alliance in 1886 which declared that "the Alliance, while not a partisan association, is political in the sense that it seeks to correct the evils of misgovernment through the ballot-box," and called upon all the producers of the State "to unite with us at the ballot-box next November to secure a legislature that will work in the interests of the many against the exactions of the few." The specific demands included state regulation of railroads, free coinage of silver, reduction of the tariff to a revenue basis, revision of the patent laws, high taxation of oleomargarine, and reduction of the legal rate of interest from 10 to 8 per cent. The secretary was directed to forward copies of these resolutions to federal and state officers and to the delegation of the State in Congress; and the members of local alliances were "urged to submit this platform of principles to every candidate for the legislature in their respective districts, and to vote as a unit against every man who refuses to publicly subscribe his name to the same and pledge himself, if elected, to live up to it."

The resolutions adopted by the National Alliance in 1887 show that the political purposes of the order had become considerably more comprehensive than they were when it was getting under way in 1881. First place was now given to a plank favoring the free coinage of silver and the issuance of "all paper money direct to the people." The demand for railroad regulation was accompanied by a statement that "the ultimate solution of the transportation problem may be found in the ownership and operation by the Government of one or more transcontinental lines"; and the immediate acquisition of the Union Pacific, then in financial difficulties, was suggested. Other resolutions called for government ownership and operation of the telegraph, improvement of waterways, restriction of the liquor traffic, industrial education in the public schools, restoration of agricultural colleges "to the high purpose of their creation," and popular election of Senators. The national body does not appear to have attempted, at this time, to force its platform upon candidates for office; but it urged "farmers throughout the country to aid in the work of immediate organization, that we may act in concert for our own and the common good."

The culmination of this general movement for

the organization of the farmers of the country came in 1889 and 1890. The Farmers' and Laborers' Union and the Northwestern Alliance met at St. Louis on December 3, 1889. The meeting of the Southern organization, which was renamed the National Farmers' Alliance and Industrial Union, was attended by about a hundred delegates representing Indiana, Kansas, and every Southern State from Maryland to Texas, with the exception of West Virginia. The purpose of the two orders in holding their meetings at the same time and place was obviously to effect some sort of union, and committees of conference were at once appointed. Difficulties soon confronted these committees: the Southern Alliance wanted to effect a complete merger but insisted upon retention of the secret features and the exclusion of negroes, at least from the national body; the Northwestern Alliance preferred a federation in which each organization might retain its identity. Arrangements were finally made for future conferences to effect federation but nothing came of them. The real obstacles seem to have been differences of policy with reference to political activity and a survival of sectional feeling.

With the failure of the movement for union, the

Southern Alliance began active work in the Northern States; and when the Supreme Council, as the national body was now called, held its next meeting at Ocala, Florida, in December, 1890, delegates were present from state alliances of seven Northern and Western States, in addition to those represented at the St. Louis meeting. The Farmers' Mutual Benefit Association, a secret order with about two hundred thousand members, had a committee in attendance at this meeting, and the Colored Farmers' Alliance, which had been founded in Texas in 1886 and claimed a membership of over a million, held its national meeting at the same time and place. Plans were formulated for a federation of these three bodies, and of such other farmers' and laborers' associations as might join with them, to the end that all might work unitedly for legislation in the interests of the industrial classes.

Signs of approaching dissolution of the Alliance movement were already apparent at the Ocala meeting. The finances of the Southern Alliance had been so badly managed that there was a deficit of about $6000 in the treasury of the Supreme Council. This was due in part to reckless expenditure and in part to difficulties in collecting dues from the state organizations. Discord had arisen, moreover, from the political campaign of 1890, and an investigating committee expressed its disapproval of the actions of the officers in connection with a senatorial contest in Georgia.   The decline of the Southern Alliance after 1890 was even more rapid than that of the Grange had been.   The failure of many of the coöperative ventures contributed to this decline; but complications and dissensions resulting from the establishment of a new political party which took over the Alliance platform, were principally responsible.   The Northwestern Alliance continued for a few years, practically as an adjunct to the new party but it, too, lost rapidly in membership and influence.   With the year 1890 interest shifts from social to political organization, from Alliances to Populism.

CHAPTER IX

THE PEOPLE'S PARTY LAUNCHED

ALLIANCES, wheels, leagues — all the agrarian organizations which multiplied during the eighties — gave tangible form to the underlying unrest created by the economic conditions of that superficially prosperous decade. Only slowly, however, did there develop a feeling that a new political party was necessary in order to apply the remedies which, it was believed, would cure some if not all the ills of the agricultural class. Old party ties were still strong. Only with reluctance could the Republican or Democrat of long standing bring himself to depart from the familiar fold. Then, too, the recent ignominious failures of the Greenback party might well cool the ardor of all but the most sanguine advocates of a third party movement. Among the leaders of the agrarian organizations were many, moreover, who foresaw that to become involved in partisan politics

125

could mean nothing less than the defeat of all their original purposes.

One disappointment after another, however, made it apparent that little was to be expected from the Republican or the Democratic party. Trust in individual politicians proved equally vain, since promises easily made during a hot campaign were as easily forgotten after the battle was over. One speaker before a state convention of the Northwest Alliance put into words what many were thinking: "There may be some contingencies when you may have to act politically. If other parties will not nominate men friendly to your interest, then your influence will have to be felt in some way or you may as well disband. If all parties nominate your enemies, then put some of your own friends into the race and then stand by them as a Christian stands by his religion." In other words, if nothing was to be gained by scattering votes among the candidates of the old parties, independent action remained the only course. Hence it was that the late eighties saw the beginnings of another party of protest, dominated by the farmers and so formidable as to cause the machine politicians to realize that a new force was abroad in the land.

After the Greenback party lost the place it had
for a fleeting moment obtained, labor once more
essayed the rôle of a third party.   In 1886, for instance, the Knights of Labor and the trades unions,
for once coöperating harmoniously, joined forces
locally with the moribund Greenbackers and with
farmers' organizations and won notable successes
at the polls in various parts of the Union, particularly in the Middle Atlantic and Western States.
Emboldened by such victories, the discontented
farmers were induced to cast in their lot with labor;
and for the next few years, the nation saw the manifestoes of a party which combined the demands of
labor and agriculture in platforms constructed not
unlike a crazy-quilt, with Henry George, James
Buchanan, and Alson J. Streeter presiding at the
sewing-bee and attempting to fit into the patch-
work the diverse and frequently clashing shades of
opinion represented in the party.   In 1888, Streeter, ex-president of the Northwestern Alliance, was
nominated for President on the Union Labor ticket
and received 146,935 votes in 27 of the 38 States.
Despite its name and some support from the Eastern workers, the new party was predominantly
Western: more than half of its total vote was polled
in Kansas, Texas, Missouri, and Arkansas.   In the

local elections of 1889 and 1890 the party still appeared but was obviously passing off the stage to make way for a greater attraction.

The meager vote for Streeter in 1888 demonstrated that the organized farmers were yet far from accepting the idea of separate political action. President Macune of the Southern Alliance probably voiced the sentiments of most of that order when he said in his address to the delegates at Shreveport in 1887: "Let the Alliance be a business organization for business purposes, and as such, necessarily secret, and as secret, necessarily non-political."[1] Even the Northwestern Alliance had given no sign of official approval to the political party in which so many of its own members played a conspicuous part.

But after the election of 1888, those who had continued to put their trust in non-political organizations gradually awoke to the fact that neither fulminations against transportation abuses, monopolies, and the protective tariff, nor the lobbying of the Southern Alliance in Washington had produced reforms. Even Macune was moved to say at

[1] At the next annual meeting, in December, 1888, no change in policy was enunciated: the plan for a national organ, unanimously adopted by the Alliance, provided that it should be "strictly non-partisan in politics and non-sectarian in religion."

HENRY GEORGE

Photograph by Gutekunst, Philadelphia.

Gravure, Anderson-Lamb Co. N.Y.

the St. Louis session in December, 1889: "We have reached a period in the history of our Government when confidence in our political leaders and great political organizations is almost destroyed, and estrangement between them and the people is becoming more manifest every day." Yet the formation of a new party under the auspices of the Alliance was probably not contemplated at this time, except possibly as a last resort, for the Alliance agreed to "support for office only such men as can be depended upon to enact these principles into statute laws, uninfluenced by party caucus." Although the demands framed at this St. Louis convention read like a party platform and, indeed, became the basis of the platform of the People's Party in 1892, they were little more than a restatement of earlier programs put forth by the Alliance and the Wheel. They called for the substitution of greenbacks for national bank notes, laws to "prevent the dealing in futures of all agricultural and mechanical productions," free and unlimited coinage of silver, prohibition of alien ownership of land, reclamation from the railroads of lands held by them in excess of actual needs, reduction and equalization of taxation, the issue of fractional paper currency for use in the mails, and, finally, government ownership

9

and operation of the means of communication and transportation.

The real contribution which this meeting made to the agrarian movement was contained in the report of the committee on the monetary system, of which C. W. Macune was chairman. This was the famous sub-treasury scheme, soon to become the paramount issue with the Alliance and the Populists in the South and in some parts of the West. The committee proposed "that the system of using certain banks as United States depositories be abolished, and in place of said system, establish in every county in each of the States that offers for sale during the one year $500,000 worth of farm products — including wheat, corn, oats, barley, rye, rice, tobacco, cotton, wool, and sugar, all together — a sub-treasury office." In connection with this office there were to be warehouses or elevators in which the farmers might deposit their crops, receiving a certificate of the deposit showing the amount and quality, and a loan of United States legal tender paper equal to eighty per cent of the local current value of the products deposited. The interest on this loan was to be at the rate of one per cent per annum; and the farmer, or the person to whom he might sell his certificate, was to be allowed one year in which to redeem the property; otherwise it would be sold at public auction for the satisfaction of the debt.   This project was expected to benefit the farmers in two ways: it would increase and make flexible the volume of currency in circulation; and it would enable them to hold their crops in anticipation of a rise in price.

The Northwestern Alliance also hesitated to play the rôle of a third party, but it adopted a program which was virtually a party platform.   In place of the sub-treasury scheme as a means of increasing the volume of currency in circulation and at the same time enabling the farmer to borrow money at low rates of interest, this organization favored the establishment of a land loan bureau operated by the Government.   Legal tender currency to the amount of $100,000,000 or more if necessary, was to be placed at the disposal of this bureau for loans upon the security of agricultural land in amounts not to exceed one-half the value of the land and at an interest rate of two per cent per annum. These loans might run for twenty years but were to be payable at any time at the option of the borrower.

With two strong organizations assuming all the functions of political parties, except the nomination of candidates, the stage was set in 1890 for a drama of unusual interest.   One scene was laid in Washington, where in the House and Senate and in the lobbies the sub-treasury scheme was aired and argued.   Lending their strength to the men from the mining States, the Alliance men aided the passage of the Silver Purchase Act, the nearest approach to free silver which Congress could be induced to make.   By the familiar practice of "log-rolling," the silverites prevented the passage of the McKinley tariff bill until the manufacturers of the East were willing to yield in part their objections to silver legislation.   But both the tariff and the silver bill seemed to the angry farmers of the West mere bones thrown to the dog under the table. They had demanded *free* silver and had secured a mere increase in the amount to be purchased; they had called for a downward revision of the duties upon manufactured products and had been given more or less meaningless "protection" of their farm produce; they had insisted upon adequate control of the trusts and had been presented with the Sherman Act, a law which might or might not curb the monopolies under which they believed themselves crushed.   All the unrest which had been gathering during the previous decade, all the venom which had been distilled by fourteen cent corn and ten per cent interest, all the blind striving to frustrate the industrial consolidation which the farmer did not understand but feared and hated, found expression in the political campaign of 1890.

The Alliance suited its political activities to local necessities. In many of the Southern States, notably Florida, Georgia, and the Carolinas, Alliance men took possession of the Democratic conventions and forced both the incorporation of their demands into the platforms and the nomination of candidates who agreed to support those demands. The result was the control of the legislatures of five Southern States by members or supporters of the order and the election of three governors, one United States Senator, and forty-four Congressmen who championed the principles of the Alliance. In the West the Alliance worked by itself and, instead of dominating an old party, created a new one. It is true that the order did not formally become a political party; but its officers took the lead in organizing People's, Independent, or Industrial parties in the different States, the membership of which was nearly identical with that of the Alliance. Nor was the farmer alone in his efforts. Throughout the whole country the prices of manufactured articles had suddenly risen, and popular opinion, fastening upon the McKinley tariff as the cause, manifested itself in a widespread desire to punish the Republican party.

The events of 1890 constituted not only a political revolt but a social upheaval in the West. Nowhere was the overturn more complete than in Kansas. If the West in general was uneasy, Kansas was in the throes of a mighty convulsion; it was swept as by the combination of a tornado and a prairie fire. As a sympathetic commentator of later days puts it, "It was a religious revival, a crusade, a pentecost of politics in which a tongue of flame sat upon every man, and each spake as the spirit gave him utterance."[1] All over the State, meetings were held in schoolhouses, churches, and public halls. Alliance picnics were all-day expositions of the doctrines of the People's Party. Up and down the State, and from Kansas City to Sharon Springs, Mary Elizabeth Lease, "Sockless" Jerry Simpson, Anna L. Diggs, William A. Peffer, Cyrus Corning, and twice a score more, were in constant demand for lectures, while lesser lights illumined the dark places when the stars of the first magnitude were scintillating elsewhere.

[1] Elizabeth N. Barr, *The Populist Uprising*, in William E. Connelly's *Standard History of Kansas and Kansans*, vol. II, p. 1148.

Mrs. Lease, who is reported to have made 160 speeches in the summer and autumn of 1890, was a curiosity in American politics.   Of Irish birth and New York upbringing, she went to Kansas and, before she was twenty years old, married Charles L. Lease.   Twelve years later she was admitted to the bar.   At the time of the campaign of 1890 she was a tall, mannish-looking, but not unattractive woman of thirty-seven years, the mother of four children.   She was characterized by her friends as refined, magnetic, and witty; by her enemies of the Republican party as a hard, unlovely shrew.   The hostile press made the most of popular prejudice against a woman stump speaker and attempted by ridicule and invective to drive her from the stage. But Mrs. Lease continued to talk.   She it was who told the Kansas farmers that what they needed was to "raise less corn and more HELL!"

Wall Street owns the country [she proclaimed]. It is no longer a government of the people, by the people, and for the people, but a government of Wall Street, by Wall Street, and for Wall Street. . . .   Money rules, and our Vice-President is a London banker.   Our laws are the output of a system that clothes rascals in robes and honesty in rags.   The parties lie to us, and the political speakers mislead us.   We were told two years ago to go to work and raise a big crop and that was all we needed. We went to work and plowed and planted; the rains fell, the sun shone, nature smiled, and we raised the big crop that they told us to; and what came of it? Eight-cent corn, ten-cent oats, two-cent beef, and no price at all for butter and eggs — that's what came of it. . . . The main question is the money question. . . . We want money, land, and transportation. We want the abolition of the National Banks, and we want the power to make loans directly from the Government. We want the accursed foreclosure system wiped out. Land equal to a tract 30 miles wide and 90 miles long has been foreclosed and bought in by loan companies of Kansas in a year. . . . The people are at bay, and the blood-hounds of money who have dogged us thus far beware!

A typical feature of this campaign in Kansas was the contest between Jerry Simpson and Colonel James R. Hallowell for a seat in Congress. Simpson nicknamed his fastidious opponent "Prince Hal" and pointed to his silk stockings as an evidence of aristocracy. Young Victor Murdock, then a cub reporter, promptly wrote a story to the effect that Simpson himself wore no socks at all. "Sockless Jerry," "Sockless Simpson," and then "Sockless Socrates" were sobriquets then and thereafter applied to the stalwart Populist. Simpson was at this time forty-eight years old, a man with a long, square-jawed face, his skin tanned by exposure on shipboard, in the army, and on the farm, and his mustache cut in a straight line over a large straight mouth. He wore clerical eyeglasses and unclerical clothes. His opponents called him clownish; his friends declared him Lincolnesque. Failing to make headway against him by ridicule, the Republicans arranged a series of joint debates between the candidates; but the audience at the first meeting was so obviously partial to Simpson that Hallowell refused to meet him again. The supporters of the "sockless" statesman, though less influential and less prosperous than those of Hallowell, proved more numerous and triumphantly elected him to Congress. In Washington he acquitted himself creditably and was perhaps disappointingly conventional in speech and attire.

The outcome of this misery, disgust, anger, and hatred on the part of the people of Kansas focused by shrewd common sense and rank demagogism, was the election of five Populist Congressmen and a large Populist majority in the lower house of the state legislature; the Republican state officers were elected by greatly reduced majorities. In Nebraska, the People's Independent party obtained a majority of the members of the legislature and reduced the Republican party to third place in the vote for governor, the victory going to the Democrats by a very small plurality. The South Dakota Independent party, with the president of the state Alliance as its standard bearer, was unable to defeat the Republican candidates for state offices but obtained the balance of power in the legislature. In Indiana, Michigan, and Minnesota, the new party movement manifested considerable strength, but, with the exception of one Alliance Congressman from Minnesota and a number of legislators, the fruits of its activity were gathered by the Democrats.

Among the results of the new party movements in the Western States in 1890 should be included the election of two United States Senators, neither of whom was a farmer, although both were ardent advocates of the farmers' cause. In South Dakota, where no one of the three parties had a majority in the legislature, the Reverend James H. Kyle, the Independent candidate, was elected to the United State Senate, when, after thirty-nine ballots, the Democrats gave him their votes. Kyle, who was only thirty-seven years old at this time, was a Congregational minister, a graduate of Oberlin College and of Alleghany Theological Seminary. He had held pastorates in Colorado and South

Dakota, and at the time of his election was financial agent for Yankton College. A radical Fourth of July oration which he delivered at Aberdeen brought him into favor with the Alliance, and he was elected to the state senate on the Independent ticket in 1890. Prior to this election Kyle had been a Republican.

The other senatorial victory was gained in Kansas, where the choice fell on William A. Peffer, whose long whiskers made him a favorite object of ridicule and caricature in Eastern papers. He was born in Pennsylvania in 1831, and as a young man had gone to California during the gold boom. Returning after two years with a considerable sum of money, he engaged in farming first in Indiana and then in Missouri. When the Civil War began, his avowed Unionist sentiments got him into trouble; and in 1862 he moved to Illinois, where after a few months he enlisted in the army. At the close of the war he settled in Tennessee and began the practice of law, which he had been studying at intervals for a number of years. He removed in 1870 to Kansas, where he played some part in politics as a Republican, was elected to the state senate, and served as a delegate to the national convention of 1880. After a number of newspaper ventures he became the editor of the *Kansas Farmer* of Topeka in 1880 and continued in that position until he was elected to the United States Senate. He was a member of the Knights of Labor and was an ardent prohibitionist and, above all, an advocate of currency inflation.

After the elections of November, 1890, came definite action in the direction of forming a new national party. The Citizens' Alliance, a secret political organization of members of the Southern Alliance, held a convention with the Knights of Labor at Cincinnati on May 19, 1891. By that time the tide of sentiment in favor of a new party was running strong. Some fourteen hundred delegates, a majority of whom were from the five States of Ohio, Kansas, Indiana, Illinois, and Nebraska, attended the convention and provided for a committee to make arrangements, in conjunction with other reform organizations if possible, for a convention of the party to nominate candidates for the presidential election of 1892. To those who were anxious to have something done immediately the process of preparing the ground for a new third party seemed long and laborious. Seen in its proper perspective, the movement now appears to have been as swift as it was inevitable. Once more, and with greater unanimity than ever before, the farmers, especially in the West, threw aside their old party allegiance to fight for the things which they deemed not only essential to their own welfare but beneficial to the whole country. Some aid, it is true, was brought by labor, some by the mining communities of the mountain region, some by various reform organizations; but the movement as a whole was distinctly and essentially agrarian.

CHAPTER X

THE advent of the Populists as a full-fledged party in the domain of national politics took place at Omaha in July, 1892. Nearly thirteen hundred delegates from all parts of the Union flocked to the convention to take part in the selection of candidates for President and Vice-President and to adopt a platform for the new party. The "Demands" of the Alliances supplied the material from which was constructed a platform characterized by one unsympathetic observer as "that furious and hysterical arraignment of the present times, that incoherent intermingling of Jeremiah and Bellamy." The document opened with a general condemnation of national conditions and a bitter denunciation of the old parties for permitting "the existing dreadful conditions to develop without serious effort to prevent or restrain them." Then followed three declarations: "that the union of the labor forces of the United States this day consummated shall be permanent and perpetual"; that "wealth belongs to him who creates it, and every dollar taken from industry without an equivalent is robbery"; and "that the time has come when the railroad corporations will either own the people or the people must own the railroads." Next came the demands.   Heading these were the monetary planks: "a national currency, safe, sound, and flexible, issued by the general Government only, a full legal tender for all debts," with the sub-treasury system of loans "or a better system; free and unlimited coinage of silver and gold at the present legal ratio of sixteen to one"; and an increase in the circulating medium until there should be not less than $50 per capita.   With demands for a graduated income tax, for honesty and economy in governmental expenditures, and for postal savings banks, the financial part of the platform was complete.   The usual plank declaring for government ownership and control of railroads and telegraphs now included the telephone systems as well, and the land plank opposed alien ownership and demanded the return of lands held by corporations in excess of their actual needs.   Other resolutions, adopted but not included in the platform, expressed sympathy with labor's demands for shorter hours, condemned the use of Pinkerton detectives in labor strife, and favored greater restriction of immigration, the initiative and referendum, direct election of United States senators, and one term for the President and Vice-President.

The platform, according to a news dispatch of the time, was "received with tremendous enthusiasm . . . and was read and adopted almost before the people knew it was read. Instantly there was enacted the mightiest scene ever witnessed by the human race. Fifteen thousand people yelled, shrieked, threw papers, hats, fans, and parasols, gathered up banners, mounted shoulders. Mrs. Lease's little girl was mounted on Dr. Fish's shoulders — he on a table on the high platform. The two bands were swamped with noise. . . . Five minutes passed, ten minutes, twenty, still the noise and hurrahs poured from hoarse throats." After forty minutes the demonstration died out and the convention was ready to proceed with the nomination of a presidential candidate.

No such unanimity marked this further procedure, however. Just before the convention the leaders of the People's Party had thrown the old parties into consternation by announcing that

Judge Walter Q. Gresham, of Indiana, would be offered the nomination. Judge Gresham, a Republican with a long and honorable public record, had been urged upon the Republican party in 1884 and 1888, and "Anti-Monopolists" had considered him with favor on account of his opinions and decisions regarding the operation and control of railroads. Just after the adoption of the platform a telegram from the judge announced that he would accept a unanimous nomination. Since unanimity was unobtainable, however, his name was withdrawn later in the day.

This left the field to General James B. Weaver of Iowa and Senator James H. Kyle of South Dakota. Weaver represented the more conservative of the Populists, the old Alliance men. His rival had the support of the most radical element as well as that of the silver men from the mountain States. The silverites were not inclined to insist upon their man, however, declaring that, if the platform contained the silver plank, they would carry their States for whatever candidate might be chosen. The old campaigner proved the stronger, and he was nominated with General James G. Field of Virginia for Vice-President. Unprejudiced observers viewed Weaver's nomination as a tactical error on the part of the Populist leaders: "Mr. Weaver has belonged to the group of third-party 'come-outers' for so many years that his name is not one to conjure with in either of the old camps; . . . his name suggests too strongly the abortive third-party movements of the past to excite much hope or enthusiasm. He is not exactly the sort of a Moses who can frighten Pharaoh into fits or bring convincing plagues upon the monopolistic oppressors of Israel. The wicked politicians of the Republican and Democratic parties breathed easier and ate with better appetites when the Gresham bogie disappeared and they found their familiar old enemy, General Weaver, in the lead of the People's movement."

It may be suspected, however, that even with Weaver at its head this party, which claimed to control from two to three million votes, and which expected to draw heavily from the discontented ranks of the old-line organizations, was not viewed with absolute equanimity by the campaign managers of Cleveland and of Harrison. Some little evidence of the perturbation appeared in the equivocal attitude of both the old parties with respect to the silver question. Said the Democratic platform: "We hold to the use of both gold and silver as the standard money of the country, and to the coinage of both gold and silver without discrimination against either metal or charge for mintage." The rival Republican platform declared that "the American people, from tradition and interest, favor bimetallism, and the Republican party demands the use of both gold and silver as standard money." Each party declared for steps to obtain an international agreement on the question. The Republicans attempted to throw a sop to the labor vote by favoring restriction of immigration and laws for the protection of employees in dangerous occupations, and to the farmer by pronouncements against trusts, for extended postal service — particularly in rural districts — and for the reclamation and sale of arid lands to settlers. The Democrats went even further and demanded the return of "nearly one hundred million acres of valuable land" then held by "corporations and syndicates, alien and domestic."

The directors of the Populist campaign proved to be no mean political strategists. General Weaver himself toured the country, accompanied by General Field when he was in the South and by Mrs. Lease when he went to the Pacific coast. Numerous other men and women addressed the thousands who attended the meetings, great and small, all over the country. One unique feature of the Populist campaign on the Pacific coast was the singing of James G. Clark's *People's Battle-Hymn*, and other songs expressing the hope and fears of labor in the field and factory. Everywhere it was the policy of the new party to enlist the assistance of the weaker of the old parties. In the South, the Populists, as a rule, arrayed themselves with the Republicans against the old Democracy. This provoked every device of ridicule, class prejudice, and scorn, which the dominant party could bring to bear to dissuade former Democrats from voting the People's ticket. One Louisiana paper uttered this warning:

Oily-tongued orators, in many cases the paid agents of the Republican party, have for months been circulating among the unsophisticated and more credulous classes, preaching their heresies and teaching the people that if Weaver is elected president, money may be had for the asking, transportation on the railroad trains will be practically free, the laboring man will be transferred from his present position and placed upon a throne of power, while lakes filled with molasses, whose shores are fringed with buckwheat cakes, and islands of Jersey butter rising here and there above the surface, will be a concomitant of every farm. The "forty-acres-and-a-mule" promises of the reconstruction era pale into insignificance beside the glowing pictures of prosperity promised by the average Populist orator to those who support Weaver.

The *Pensacola Address* of the Populist nominees on September 17, 1892, which served as a joint letter of acceptance, was evidently issued at that place and time partly for the purpose of influencing such voters as might be won over by emphasizing the unquestioned economic distress of most Southern farmers. If the new party could substantiate the charges that both old parties were the tools of monopoly and Wall Street, it might insert the wedge which would eventually split the "solid South." Even before the *Pensacola Address*, the state elections in Alabama and Arkansas demonstrated that coöperation of Republicans with Populists was not an idle dream. But, although fusion was effected on state tickets in several States in the November elections, the outcome was the choice of Cleveland electors throughout the South.

As the Populists tried in the South to win over the Republicans, so in the North and more especially the West they sought to control the Democratic vote either by fusion or absorption. The effort was so successful that in Colorado, Idaho, Kansas, Nevada, and North Dakota, the new party swept the field with the assistance of the Democrats. In South Dakota and Nebraska, where there was no fusion, the Democratic vote was negligible and the Populists ran a close second to the Republicans.

That the tide of agrarianism was gradually flowing westward as the frontier advanced is apparent from the election returns in the States bordering on the upper Mississippi. Iowa and Missouri, where the Alliance had been strong, experienced none of the landslide which swept out the Republicans in States further west. In Minnesota the Populists, with a ticket headed by the veteran Donnelly, ran a poor third in the state election, and the entire Harrison electoral ticket was victorious in spite of the endorsement of four Populist candidates by the Democrats. In the northwestern part of the State, however, the new party was strong enough to elect a Congressman over candidates of both the old parties. In no Northern State east of the Mississippi were the Populists able to make a strong showing; but in Illinois, the success of John P. Altgeld, the Democratic candidate for governor, was due largely to his advocacy of many of the measures demanded by the People's party, particularly those relating to labor, and to the support which he received from the elements which might have been expected to aline themselves with the Populists. On the Pacific coast, despite the musical campaign of Clark, Mrs. Lease, and Weaver, California proved deaf to the People's cause; but in Oregon the party stood second in the lists and in Washington it ran a strong third.

More than a million votes, nearly nine per cent of the total, were cast for the Populist candidates in this election — a record for a third party the year after its birth, and one exceeded only by that of the Republican party when it appeared for the first time in the national arena in 1856. Twenty-two electoral votes added point to the showing, for hitherto, since 1860, third-party votes had been so scattered that they had affected the choice of President only as a makeweight between other parties in closely contested States.

A week after the elections General Weaver announced that the Populists had succeeded far beyond their expectations. "The Republican party," he asserted, "is as dead as the Whig party was after the Scott campaign of 1852, and from this time forward will diminish in every State of the Union and cannot make another campaign. . . . The Populist will now commence a vigorous campaign and will push the work of organization and education in every county in the Union." There were those, however, who believed that the new party had made a great mistake in having anything to do with either of the old parties, that fusion, particularly of the sort which resulted in combination tickets, was a compromise with the enemy, and that more votes had been lost than won by the process. This feeling found characteristic expression in an editorial in a Minnesota paper:

Take an audience of republican voters in a schoolhouse where a county fusion has taken place — or the press is full of the electoral deal — and the audience will applaud the sentiments of the speaker — but they wont vote a mongrel or democratic ticket! A wet blanket has been thrown!

"Oh," says someone, "but the democratic party is a party of reform!" Well, my friend, you better go down south and talk that to the peoples party where they have been robbed of their franchises by fraud and outrage!

Ah, and there the peoples party fused the republicans!!!

Oh whitewash! Where is thy lime-kiln, that we may swab off the dark blemishes of the hour!! Aye, and on the whited wall, draw thee a picture of power and beauty — Cleveland, for instance, thanking the peoples party for all the favors gratuitously granted by our mongrel saints in speckled linen and green surtouts.

As time gave perspective, however, the opinion grew that 1892 had yielded all that could possibly have been hoped. The lessons of the campaign may have been hard, but they had been learned, and, withal, a stinging barb had been thrust into the side of the Republican party, the organization which, in the minds of most crusaders, was principally responsible for the creation and nurture of their ills. It was generally determined that in the next campaign Populism should stand upon its own feet; Democratic and Republican votes should be won by conversion of individuals to the cause rather than by hybrid amalgamation of parties and pre-election agreements for dividing the spoils.   But it was just this fusion which blinded the eyes of the old party leaders to the significance of the Populist returns.   Democrats, with a clear majority of electoral votes, were not inclined to worry about local losses or to value incidental gains; and Republicans felt that the menace of the third party was much less portentous than it might have been as an independent movement.

CHAPTER XI

THE SILVER ISSUE

A REMARKABLE manifesto, dated February 22, 1895, summarized the grievances of the Populists in these words:

As early as 1865–66 a conspiracy was entered into between the gold gamblers of Europe and America to accomplish the following purposes: to fasten upon the people of the United States the burdens of perpetual debt; to destroy the greenbacks which had safely brought us through the perils of war; to strike down silver as a money metal; to deny to the people the use of Federal paper and silver — the two independent sources of money guaranteed by the Constitution; to fasten upon the country the single gold standard of Britain, and to delegate to thousands of banking corporations, organized for private gain, the sovereign control, for all time, over the issue and volume of all supplemental paper currency.

Declaring that the "international gold ring" was summoning all its powers to strike at the prosperity of the country, the authors of this address called upon Populists to take up the gauntlet and meet "the enemy upon his chosen field of battle," with the "aid and coöperation of all persons who favor the immediate free coinage of silver at a ratio of 16–1, the issue of all paper money by the Government without the intervention of banks of issue, and who are opposed to the issue of interest-bearing government bonds in the time of peace."

There was nothing new in this declaration of hostility to bank issues and interest-bearing bonds, nor in this demand for government paper money, for these prejudices and this predilection had given rise to the "Ohio idea," by force of which George H. Pendleton had hoped to achieve the presidency in 1868. These same notions had been the essence of the platforms of the Greenback party in the late seventies; and they had jostled government ownership of railroads for first place in pronunciamentos of labor and agricultural organizations and of third parties all during the eighties. Free silver, on the other hand, although not ignored in the earlier period, did not attain foremost rank among the demands of the dissatisfied classes until the last decade of the century and more particularly after the panic of 1893.

Prior to 1874 or 1875 the "silver question" did

not exist.   In 1873 Congress, moved by the report
of a commission it had authorized, had demonetized silver; that is, it had provided that the gold
dollar should be the standard of value, and omitted
the standard silver dollar from the list of silver
coins.[1]   In this consisted the "Crime of '73."   At
the time when this law was enacted it had not for
many years been profitable to coin silver bullion
into dollars because silver was undervalued at the
established ratio of sixteen to one.   In 1867 the
International Monetary Conference of Paris had
pronounced itself in favor of a single gold standard
of currency, and the principal countries of Europe
had preceded the United States in demonetizing
silver or in limiting its coinage.   In 1874 as a result of a revision of the statutes of the United
States, the existing silver dollars were reduced to
the basis of subsidiary coins with only limited legal
tender value.

The Act of 1873 was before Congress for four
sessions; every section, including that which made
gold the sole standard of value, was discussed
even by those who later claimed that the Act had
been passed surreptitiously.   Whatever opposition

[1] The only reference to the dollar was to "the trade dollar" of
heavier weight, for use in the Orient.

developed at this time was not directed against the omission of the silver dollar from the list of coins nor against the establishment of a single standard of value. The situation was quickly changed, however, by the rapid decline in the market price of silver. The bimetallists claimed that this decline was a result of the monetary changes; the advocates of the gold standard asserted that it was due to the great increase in the production of silver. Whatever the cause, the result was that, shortly after silver had been demonetized, its value in proportion to gold fell below that expressed by the ratio of sixteen to one. Under these circumstances the producers could have made a profit by taking their bullion to the mint and having it coined into dollars, if it had not been for the Act of 1873. It is not strange, therefore, that the people of those Western States whose prosperity depended largely on the silver mining industry demanded the remonetization of this metal. At the same time the stringency in the money market and the low prices following the panic of 1873 added weight to the arguments of those who favored an increase in the quantity of currency in circulation and who saw in the free and unlimited coinage of silver one means of accomplishing this end. So powerful was the demand, especially from the West, that in 1878 the Bland-Allison Act, passed over the veto of President Hayes, provided for the restoration of the silver dollar to the list of coins, with full legal tender quality, and required the Treasury to purchase in the open market from two to four million dollars' worth of bullion each month. This compromise, however, was unsatisfactory to those who desired the free coinage of silver, and it failed to please the champions of the single standard.

For ten years the question of a choice between a single standard or bimetallism, between free coinage or limited coinage of silver, was one of the principal economic problems of the world. International conferences, destined to have no positive results, met in 1878 and again in 1881; in the United States Congress read reports and debated measures on coinage in the intervals between tariff debates. Political parties were split on sectional lines: Western Republicans and Democrats alike were largely in favor of free silver, but their Eastern associates as generally took the other side. Party platforms in the different States diverged widely on this issue; and monetary planks in national platforms, if included at all, were so framed as to commit the party to neither side. Both parties, however, could safely pronounce for bimetallism under international agreement, since there was little real prospect of procuring such an agreement. The minor parties as a rule frankly advocated free silver.

In 1890, the subject of silver coinage assumed new importance. The silverites in Congress were reënforced by representatives from new States in the far West, the admission of which had not been unconnected with political exigencies on the part of the Republican party. The advocates of the change were not strong enough to force through a free-silver bill, but they were able by skillful log-rolling to bring about the passage of the Silver Purchase Act. This measure, frequently called the Sherman Law,[1] directed the Secretary of the Treasury to purchase, with legal tender Treasury notes issued for the purpose, 4,500,000 ounces of pure silver each month at the market price. As the metal was worth at that time about a dollar an ounce, this represented an increase, for the time being, over the maximum allowed under the Bland-Allison Act and more than double the minimum required by that measure, which was all the Treasury had ever

[1] John Sherman, then Secretary of Treasury, had a large share in giving final form to the bill, which he favored only for fear of a still more objectionable measure. See Sherman's *Recollections*, pp. 1069, 1188.

purchased.   But the Silver Purchase Act failed to check the downward trend in the value of the metal. The bullion in a silver dollar, which had been worth $1.02 in 1872, had declined to seventy-two cents in 1889.   It rose to seventy-six in 1891 but then declined rapidly to sixty in 1893, and during the next three years the intrinsic value of a "cartwheel" was just about half its legal tender value.

Even under the Bland-Allison Act the Treasury Department had experienced great difficulty in keeping in circulation a reasonable proportion of the silver dollars and the silver certificates which were issued in lieu of part of them, and in maintaining a sufficient gold reserve to insure the stability of the currency.   When the Silver Purchase Act went into operation, therefore, the monetary situation contributed its share to conditions which produced the panic of 1893.   Thereupon the silver issue became more than ever a matter of nation-wide discussion.

From the Atlantic to the Pacific the country was flooded with controversial writing, much of it cast in a form to make an appeal to classes which had neither the leisure nor the training to master this very intricate economic problem.   W. H. Harvey's *Coin's Financial School* was the most widely read campaign document, although hundreds of similar pamphlets and books had an enormous circulation. The pithy and plausible arguments of "Coin" and his ready answers to questions supposedly put by prominent editors, bankers, and university professors, as well as by J. R. Sovereign, master workman of the Knights of Labor, tickled the fancy of thousands of farmers who saw their own plight depicted in the crude but telling woodcuts which sprinkled the pages of the book. In his mythical school "the smooth little financier" converted to silver many who had been arguing for gold; but — what is more to the point — he also convinced hundreds of voters that gold was the weapon with which the bankers of England and America had slain silver in order to maintain high interest rates while reducing prices, and that it was the tool with which they were everywhere welding the shackles upon labor. "Coin" harped upon a string to which, down to the time of the Spanish War, most Americans were ever responsive — the conflict of interests between England and the United States. "If it is claimed," he said, "we must adopt for our money the metal England selects, and can have no independent choice in the matter, let us make the test and find out if it is true." He pointed to the nations of the earth where a silver standard ruled: "The farmer in Mexico sells his bushel of wheat for one dollar. The farmer in the United States sells his bushel of wheat for fifty cents. The former is proven by the history of the world to be an equitable price. The latter is writing its history, in letters of blood, on the appalling cloud of debt that is sweeping with ruin and desolation over the farmers of this country."

When many men of sound reputation believed the maintenance of a gold standard impossible what wonder that millions of farmers shouted with "Coin": "Give the people back their favored primary money! Give us two arms with which to transact business! Silver the right arm and gold the left arm! Silver the money of the people, and gold the money of the rich. Stop this legalized robbery that is transferring the property of the debtors to the possession of the creditors. . . . Drive these money-changers from our temples. Let them discover your aspect, their masters — the people."

The relations of the Populist party to silver were at once the result of conviction and expediency; cheap money had been one, frequently the most prominent, of the demands of the farming class, not only from the inception of the Greenback movement, as we have seen, but from the very beginning of American history. Indeed, the pioneer everywhere has needed capital and has believed that it could be obtained only through money. The cheaper the money, the better it served his needs. The Western farmer preferred, other things being equal, that the supply of currency should be increased by direct issue of paper by the Government. Things, however, were not equal. In the Mountain States were many interested in silver as a commodity whose assistance could be counted on in a campaign to increase the amount of the metal in circulation. There were, moreover, many other voters who, while regarding Greenbackism as an economic heresy, were convinced that bimetallism offered a safe and sound solution of the currency problem. For the sake of added votes the inflationists were ready to waive any preference as to the form in which the cheap money should be issued. Before the actual formation of the People's Party, the farmers' organizations had set out to capture votes by advocating free silver. After the election of 1892 free silver captured the Populist organization.

Heartened by the large vote of 1892 the Populist leaders prepared to drive the wedge further into the old parties and even hoped to send their candidates through the breach to Congress and the presidency. A secret organization, known as the Industrial League of the United States, in which the leaders were for the most part the prominent officials of the People's Party, afforded for a time through its lodges the machinery with which to control and organize the silverites of the West and the South.

The most notable triumph of 1893 was the selection of Judge William V. Allen, by the Democrats and Independents of Nebraska, to represent that State in the United States Senate. Born in Ohio, in a house which had been a station on the "underground railroad" to assist escaping negroes, Allen at ten years of age had gone with his family to Iowa. After one unsuccessful attempt, he enlisted in the Union Army at the age of fifteen and served from 1862 to the end of the War. When peace came, he resumed his schooling, attended college, studied law, and in 1869 was admitted to the bar. In 1884 he went to Madison County, Nebraska, where seven years later he was elected district judge by the Populists. Reared in a family which had been Republican, he himself had supported this party until the campaign of 1890. "I have always," said he, "looked upon a political party . . .

simply as a means to an end. I think a party should be held no more sacred than a man's shoes or garments, and that whenever it fails to subserve the purposes of good government a man should abandon it as cheerfully as he dispenses with his wornout clothes." As Senator, Allen attracted attention not only by his powers of physical endurance as attested by a fifteen-hour speech in opposition to the bill for the repeal of the Silver Purchase Act, but also by his integrity of character. "If Populism can produce men of Senator Allen's mold," was the comment of one Eastern review, "and then lift them into positions of the highest responsibility, one might be tempted to suggest that an epidemic of this Western malady would prove beneficial to some Eastern communities and have salutary results for the nation at large."

In this same year (1893) Kansas became a storm-center in national politics once more by reason of a contest between parties for control of the lower house of the legislature. The returns had given the Republicans a majority in the assembly, but several Republican seats had been contested on suspicion of fraud. If the holders of these seats were debarred from voting, the Populists could outvote the Republicans. The situation itself was fraught with comedy; and the actions of the contestants made it nothing less than farce. The assembly convened on the 10th of January, and both Republican and Populist speakers were declared duly elected by their respective factions. Loftily ignoring each other, the two speakers went to the desk and attempted to conduct the business of the house. Neither party left the assembly chamber that night; the members slept on the benches; the speakers called a truce at two in the morning, and lay down, gavels in hand, facing each other behind the desk, to get what rest they could. For over two weeks the two houses continued in tumultuous session. Meanwhile men were crowding into Topeka from all over the State: grim-faced Populist farmers, determined that Republican chicanery should not wrest from them the fruits of the election; equally determined Republicans, resolved that the Populists should not, by charges of election fraud, rob them of their hard-won majority. Both sides came armed but apparently hoping to avoid bloodshed.

Finally, on the 15th of February, the Populist house retreated from the chamber, leaving the Republicans in possession, and proceeded to transact business of state in the corridor of the Capitol.

Populist sympathizers now besieged the assembly chamber, immuring the luckless Republicans and incidentally a few women who had come in as members of the suffrage lobby and were now getting more of political equality than they had anticipated. Food had to be sent through the Populist lines in baskets, or drawn up to the windows of the chamber while the Populist mob sat on the main stairway within. Towards evening, the Populist janitor turned off the heat; and the Republicans shivered until oil stoves were fetched by their followers outside and hoisted through the windows. The Republican sheriff swore in men of his party as special deputies; the Populist governor called out the militia.

The situation was at once too absurd and too grave to be permitted to continue. "Sockless" Jerry Simpson now counseled the Populists to let the decision go to the courts. The judges, to be sure, were Republican; but Simpson, ever resourceful, argued that if they decided against the Populists, the house and senate could then impeach them. Mrs. Lease, however, was sure that the Populists would not have the courage to take up impeachment proceedings, and the event proved her judgment correct. When the struggle was finally brought to an end with the assistance of the judicial machinery, the Republicans were left in control of the house of representatives, while the Populists retained the senate. In joint session the Republicans could be outvoted; hence a silver Democrat, John Martin, was sent to Washington to work with Peffer in the Senate for the common cause of silver.

The congressional and state elections of 1894 revealed the unstable equilibrium of parties, and at the same time the total Populist vote of nearly a million and a half reflected the increasing popular unrest. In the West, however, the new party was not so successful in winning elections as it had been in 1892 because the hostile attitude, sometimes of the Populists and sometimes of the Democrats, made fusion impossible in most cases. A few victories were won, to be sure: Nebraska elected a free-silver Democrat-Populist governor, while Nevada was carried by the silver party; but Colorado, Idaho, Wyoming, Kansas, and North Dakota returned to the Republican fold. In the South, the fusion between Populists and Republicans against the dominant Democrats was more successful. From several States, Congressmen were elected, who, whether under the name of Populist or

Republican, represented the radical element. In South Carolina the Democratic party adopted the Farmers' Alliance platform, swept the State in the elections, and sent "Pitchfork" Tillman to the United States Senate as an anti-administration Democrat. Tillman admitted that he was not one of those infatuated persons who believed that "all the financial wisdom in the country is monopolized by the East," and who said, "'Me, too,' every time Cleveland grunts." "Send me to Washington," was his advice to cheering crowds, "and I'll stick my pitchfork into his old ribs!"

Every political move in 1895 was calculated with reference to the presidential election of 1896. Both old parties were inoculated with the free-silver virus; silver men could have passed a free coinage bill in both houses of Congress at any moment but were restrained chiefly by the knowledge that such a measure would be vetoed by President Cleveland. The free coinage of silver, which was the chief demand of Populism, was also the ardent desire of a majority of the people west of the Alleghanies, irrespective of their political affiliations. Nothing seemed more logical, then, than the union of all silver men to enforce the adoption of their program. There was great diversity of opinion, however, as to the best means of accomplishing this union.   General Weaver started a movement to add the forces of the American Bimetallic League and the silver Democrats to the ranks of the People's Party.   But the silver Democrats, believing that they comprised a majority of the party, proceeded to organize themselves for the purpose of controlling that party at its coming national conventions; and most of the Populist leaders felt that, should this movement be victorious, the greatest prospect of success for their program lay in a fusion of the two parties.   Some there were, indeed, who opposed fusion under any conditions, foreseeing that it would mean the eventual extinction of the People's Party.   Prominent among these were Ignatius Donnelly of Minnesota, "General" J. S. Coxey of Ohio, and Senator Peffer of Kansas.   In the South the "middle-of-the-road" element, as the opponents of fusion were called, was especially strong, for there the Populists had been coöperating with the Republicans since 1892, and not even agreement on the silver issue could break down the barrier of antagonism between them and the old-line Democrats.

It remained, then, for the political events of 1896 to decide which way the current of Populism would flow — whether it would maintain an independent course, receiving tributaries from every political source, eventually becoming a mighty river, and, like the Republican party of 1856 and 1860, sweeping away an older party; or whether it would turn aside and mingle with the stream of Democracy, there to lose its identity forever.

CHAPTER XII

WHEN the Republicans met in convention at St. Louis in the middle of June, 1896, the monetary issue had already dwarfed all other political questions. It was indeed the rock on which the party might have crashed in utter shipwreck but for the precautions of one man who had charted the angry waters and the dangerous shoals and who now had a firm grasp on the helm. Marcus A. Hanna, or "Uncle Mark," was the genial owner of more mines, oil wells, street railways, aldermen, and legislators than any other man in Ohio. Hanna was an almost perfect example of what the Populists denounced as the capitalist in politics. Cynically declaring that "no man in public life owes the public anything," he had gone his unscrupulous way, getting control of the political machine of Cleveland, acquiring influence in the state legislature, and now even assuming dictatorship over the national Republican party.   Because he had found that political power was helpful in the prosecution of his vast business enterprises, he went forth to accumulate political power, just as frankly as he would have gone to buy the machinery for pumping oil from one of his wells.   Hanna was a stanch friend of the gold standard, but he was too clever to alienate the sympathies of the Republican silverites by supporting the nomination of a man known to be an uncompromising advocate of gold.   He chose a safer candidate, a man whose character he sincerely admired and whose opinions he might resonably expect to sway — his personal friend, Major William McKinley.   This was a clever choice: McKinley was known to the public largely as the author of the McKinley tariff bill; his protectionism pleased the East; and what was known of his attitude on the currency question did not offend the West.   In Congress he had voted for the Bland-Allison bill and had advocated the freer use of silver.   McKinley was, indeed, an ideally "safe" candidate, an upright, affable gentleman whose aquiline features conferred on him the semblance of commanding power and masked the essential weakness and indecision which would make him, from Mark Hanna's point of view, a desirable

President. McKinley would always swim with the tide.

In his friend's behalf Hanna carried on a shrewd campaign in the newspapers, keeping the question of currency in the background as far as possible, playing up McKinley's sound tariff policy, and repeating often the slogan — welcome after the recent lean years — "McKinley and the full dinner pail." McKinley prudently refused to take any stand on the currency question, protesting that he could not anticipate the party platform and that he would be bound by whatever declarations the party might see fit to make. Even after the convention had opened, McKinley and Hanna were reticent on the silver question. Finally, fearing that some kind of compromise would be made, the advocates of the gold standard went to Mr. Hanna and demanded that a gold plank be incorporated in the platform. Hanna gracefully acceded to their demands and thus put them under obligation to repay him by supporting McKinley for the nomination. The platform which was forthwith reported to the convention contained the unequivocal gold plank, as Hanna had long before planned. Immediately thereafter a minority of thirty-four delegates, led by Senator Teller of Colorado, left the convention, later to send out an address advising all Republicans who believed in free coinage of silver to support the Democratic ticket. The nomination of William McKinley and Garret A. Hobart followed with very little opposition.

There was nothing cut and dried about the Democratic convention which assembled three weeks later in Chicago. The Northeastern States and a few others sent delegations in favor of the gold standard, but free silver and the West were in the saddle. This was demonstrated when, in the face of all precedent, the nominee of the national committee for temporary chairman was rejected in favor of Senator John W. Daniel of Virginia, a strong silver man. The second day of the convention saw the advantage pushed further: each Territory had its representation increased threefold; of contesting delegations those who represented the gold element in their respective States were unseated to make way for silverites; and Stephen M. White, one of the California senators, was made permanent chairman.

On the third day of the convention the platform, devoted largely to the money question, was the subject of bitter debate. "We are unalterably opposed to monometallism, which has locked fast the prosperity of an industrial people in the paralysis of hard times," proclaimed the report of the committee on resolutions. "Gold monometallism is a British policy, and its adoption has brought other nations into financial servitude to London. . . . We demand the free and unlimited coinage of both gold and silver at the present legal ratio of sixteen to one without waiting for the aid or consent of any other nation." A minority of the committee on resolutions proposed two amendments to the report, one pronouncing in favor of a gold standard, and the other commending the record of Grover Cleveland, a courtesy always extended to a presidential incumbent of the same party. At the name of Cleveland, Senator Tillman leaped to his feet and delivered himself of characteristic invective against the President, the "tool of Wall Street," the abject slave of gold. Senator David B. Hill of New York, who had been rejected for temporary chairman, defended the gold plank in a logical analysis of monetary principles. But logical analysis could not prevail against emotion; that clamorous mass of men was past reasoning now, borne they hardly knew whither on the current of their own excitement. He might as well have tried to dam Niagara.

WILLIAM JENNINGS BRYAN

Photograph by Pach Bros., New York, 1896.

Bravura, Andersen-Lamb Co. N.Y.

Others tried to stem the onrushing tide but with no better success.   It seemed to be impossible for any one to command the attention and respect of that tumultuous gathering.   Even Senator James K. Jones of Arkansas, a member of the majority group of the committee on resolutions, failed equally with Tillman to give satisfactory expression to the sentiments of that convention, which felt inchoately what it desired but which still needed a leader to voice its aspirations.   This spokesman the convention now found in William Jennings Bryan, to whom after a few sentences Senator Jones yielded the floor.

Bryan appeared in Chicago as a member of the contesting silver delegation from Nebraska. A young man, barely thirty-six years old, he had already become a well-known figure in the West, where for years he had been expounding the doctrine of free silver.   A native of Illinois, whither his father had come from Culpeper County, Virginia, Bryan had grown up on a farm. His father's means had been ample to afford him a good education, which he completed, so far as schooling was concerned, at Illinois College, Jacksonville, and at the Union College of Law in Chicago.   While in Chicago Bryan was employed in the law office of

12

Lyman Trumbull, one of the stanchest representatives of independence in politics — an independence which had caused him to break with the Democratic party over the slavery issue, and which, as expressed in his vote against the impeachment of President Johnson, had resulted in his retirement to private life. To the young law student Trumbull took a particular fancy, and his dominating personality exerted an abiding influence over the character and career of his protégé.

After a brief period of law practice in Jacksonville, Illinois, Bryan removed with his family to Lincoln, Nebraska. The legal profession never held great attraction for him, despite the encouragement and assistance of his wife, who herself took up the study of law after her marriage and was admitted to the bar. Public questions and politics held greater interest for the young man, who had already, in his college career, shown his ability as an orator. Nebraska offered the opportunity he craved. At the Democratic state convention in Omaha in 1888 he made a speech on the tariff which gave him immediately a state-wide reputation as an orator and expounder of public issues. He took an active part in the campaign of that year, and in 1889 was offered, but declined, the nomination for lieutenant governor on the Democratic ticket.   In 1890 he won election to Congress by a majority of seven thousand in a district which two years before had returned a Republican, and this he accomplished in spite of the neglect of party managers who regarded the district as hopeless. In Congress he became a member of the Committee on Ways and Means.   On the floor of the House his formal speeches on the tariff, a topic to which nothing new could be brought, commanded the attention of one of the most critical and blasé audiences of the world.   The silver question, which was the principal topic before Congress at the following session, afforded a fresher field for his oratory; indeed, Bryan was the principal aid to Bland both as speaker and parliamentarian in the old leader's monetary campaign.   When Bryan sat down after a three-hour speech in which he attacked the gold standard, a colleague remarked, "It exhausts the subject."   In 1894 a tidal wave of Republicanism destroyed Bryan's chances of being elected United States Senator, a consummation for which he had been laboring on the stump and, for a brief period, as editor of the Omaha *World-Herald*. He continued, however, to urge the silver cause in preparation for the presidential campaign of 1896.

Taller and broader than most men and of more
commanding presence, Bryan was a striking figure
in the convention hall. He wore the inevitable
black suit of the professional man of the nineties,
but his dress did not seem conventional: his black
tie sat at too careless an angle; his black hair was a
little too long.   These eccentricities the cartoonists
seized on and exaggerated so that most people who
have not seen the man picture Bryan, not as a determined looking man with a piercing eye and tight-
set mouth, but as a grotesque frock-coated figure
with the sombrero of a cow-puncher and the hair
of a poet. If the delegates at the convention noticed
any of these peculiarities as Bryan arose to speak,
they soon forgot them. His undoubted power
to carry an audience with him was never better
demonstrated than on that sweltering July day in
Chicago when he stilled the tumult of a seething
mass of 15,000 people with his announcement that
he came to speak "in defense of a cause as holy as
the cause of liberty — the cause of humanity," and
when he stirred the same audience to frenzy with
his closing defiance of the opponents of free silver:

If they say bimetallism is good, but that we cannot have
it until other nations help us, we reply that, instead of
having a gold standard because England has, we will

restore bimetallism, and then let England have bimetallism because the United States has it. If they dare to
come out in the open field and defend the gold standard as a good thing, we will fight them to the utter-
most. Having behind us the producing masses of this
nation and the world, supported by the commercial
interests, the laboring interests, and the toilers everywhere, we will answer their demand for a gold standard
by saying to them: You shall not press down upon
the brow of labor this crown of thorns, you shall not
crucify mankind upon a cross of gold.

Meeting Senator Hill's careful arguments with
a clever retort, blunting the keenness of his logic
with a well-turned period, polished to perfection
by numerous repetitions before all sorts of audiences during the previous three or four years, Bryan held the convention in the hollow of his hand.
The leadership which had hitherto been lacking
was now found. The platform as reported by the
committee was adopted by a vote of more than
two to one; and the convention, but for the opposition of Bryan himself, would have nominated him
on the spot. The next day it took but five ballots
to set aside all the favorite sons, including the
"Father of Free Silver" himself, Richard P. Bland,
and to make Bryan the standard bearer of the party.

Far different in character and appearance from

the Republican group which had assembled in the same building a few weeks before, was the Populist convention which met in St. Louis late in July. Many of the 1300 delegates were white-haired and had grown old in the service of reform in the various independent movements of preceding years; some of them had walked long distances to save railroad fare, while others were so poor that, having exhausted their small store of money before the long-drawn-out convention adjourned, they suffered from want of regular sleeping places and adequate food. All were impressed with the significance of the decision they must make.

Gone were the hopes of the past months; the Populist party would not sweep into its ranks all anti-monopolists and all silverites — for one of the old parties had stolen its loudest thunder! It was an error of political strategy to place the convention after those of the two great parties in the expectation that both would stand on a gold platform. Now it was for these delegates to decide whether they would put their organization behind the Democratic nominee with a substantial prospect of victory, or preserve intact the identity of the Populist party, split the silver vote, and deliver over the election to a gold Republican.

The majority of the delegates, believing that the Democratic party had been inoculated with the serum of reform, were ready for the sake of a principle to risk the destruction of the party they had labored so hard to build. Senator William V. Allen of Nebraska summed up the situation when he said:

If by putting a third ticket in the field you would defeat free coinage; defeat a withdrawal of the issue power of national banks; defeat Government ownership of railroads, telephones and telegraphs; defeat an income tax and foist gold monometallism and high taxation upon the people for a generation to come, which would you do? . . . When I shall go back to the splendid commonwealth that has so signally honored me beyond my merits, I want to be able to say to the people that all the great doctrines we have advocated for years, have been made possible by your action. I do not want them to say that the Populists have been advocates of reforms when they could not be accomplished, but when the first ray of light appeared and the people were looking with expectancy and with anxiety for relief, the party was not equal to the occasion; that it was stupid; it was blind; it kept "the middle of the road," and missed the golden opportunity.

Although most of the members of the convention were ready to coöperate with the Democrats, there was a very strong feeling that something should be done, if possible, to preserve the identity of the

Populist party and to safeguard its future.   An active minority, moreover, was opposed to any sort of fusion or coöperation. This "middle-of-the-road" group included some Western leaders of prominence, such as Peffer and Donnelly, but its main support came from the Southern delegates. To them an alliance with the Democratic party meant a surrender to the enemy, to an enemy with whom they had been struggling for four years for the control of their state and local governments. Passionately they pleaded with the convention to save them from such a calamity.   Well they knew that small consideration would be given to those who had dared stand up and oppose the ruling aristocracy of the South, who had even shaken the Democratic grip upon the governments of some of the States.   Further, a negro delegate from Georgia portrayed the disaster which would overwhelm the political aspirations of his people if the Populist party, which alone had given them full fellowship, should surrender to the Democrats.

The advocates of fusion won their first victory in the election of Senator Allen as permanent chairman, by a vote of 758 to 564.   As the nomination of Bryan for President was practically a foregone conclusion, the "middle-of-the-road" element

concentrated its energies on preventing the nomination of Arthur Sewall of Maine, the choice of the
Democracy, for Vice-President.   The convention
was persuaded, by a narrow margin, to take the
unusual step of selecting the candidate for Vice-
President before the head of the ticket was chosen.
On the first ballot Sewall received only 257 votes,
while 469 were cast for Thomas Watson of Georgia.
Watson, who was then nominated by acclamation,
was a country editor who had made himself a force
in the politics of his own State and had served the
Populist cause conspicuously in Congress.   Two
motives influenced the convention in this procedure.   As a bank president, a railroad director, and
an employer of labor on a large scale, Sewall was
felt to be utterly unsuited to carry the standard
of the People's Party.   More effective than this
feeling, however, was the desire to do something to
preserve the identity of the party, to show that it
had not wholly surrendered to the Democrats.   It
was a compromise, moreover, which was probably
necessary to prevent a bolt of the "middle-of-the-
road" element and the nomination of an entirely
independent ticket.

Even with this concession the Southern delegates
continued their opposition to fusion.   Bryan was

placed in nomination, quite appropriately, by General Weaver, who again expressed the sense of the convention: "After due consideration, in which I have fully canvassed every possible phase of the subject, I have failed to find a single good reason to justify us in placing a third ticket in the field. . . . I would not endorse the distinguished gentleman named at Chicago. I would nominate him outright, and make him our own, and then share justly and rightfully in his election." The irreconcilables, nearly all from the South and including a hundred delegates from Texas, voted for S. F. Norton of Chicago, who received 321 votes as against 1042 for Bryan.

Because of the electoral system, the agreement of two parties to support the same candidate for President could have no effect, unless arrangements were made for fusion within the States. An address issued by the executive committee of the national committee of the People's Party during the course of the campaign outlined the method of uniting "the voters of the country against McKinley," and of overcoming the "obstacles and embarrassments which, if the Democratic party had put the cause first and party second," would not have been encountered: "This could be accomplished only by arranging for a division of the electoral votes in every State possible, securing so many electors for Bryan and Watson and conceding so many to Bryan and Sewall. At the opening of the campaign this, under the circumstances, seemed the wisest course for your committee, and it is clearer today than ever that it was the only safe and wise course if your votes were to be cast and made effective for the relief of an oppressed and outraged people. Following this line of policy your committee has arranged electoral tickets in three-fourths of the States and will do all in its power to make the same arrangements in all of the States."

The committee felt it necessary to warn the people of the danger of "a certain portion of the rank and file of the People's Party being misled by so-called leaders, who, for reasons best known to themselves, or for want of reason, are advising voters to rebel against the joint electoral tickets and put up separate electoral tickets, or to withhold their support from the joint electoral tickets." Such so-called leaders were said to be aided and abetted by "Democrats of the revenue stripe, who are not yet weaned from the flesh-pots of Egypt," and by Republican "goldbugs" who in desperation were seizing upon every straw to prevent fusion and so to promote their own chances of success.

In the North and West, where the Populist had been fusing with the Democrats off and on for several years, the combinations were arranged with little difficulty.   In apportioning the places on the electoral tickets the strength of the respective parties was roughly represented by the number of places assigned to each.   Usually it was understood that all the electors, if victorious, would vote for Bryan, while the Democrats would cast their second place ballots for Sewall and the Populists for Watson.

In the South much more difficulty was experienced in arranging fusion tickets, and the spectacle of Populists coöperating with Republicans in state elections and with Democrats in the national election illustrated the truth of the adage that "politics makes strange bedfellows."   Only in Arkansas, Kentucky, Louisiana, Missouri, and North Carolina, of the Southern States, were joint electoral tickets finally agreed upon.   In Tennessee the Populists offered to support the Democratic electors if they would all promise to vote for Watson, a proposal which was naturally declined.   In Florida the chairman of the state committee of the People's

Party, went so far on the eve of the election as to advise all members of the party to vote for Mc-Kinley; and in Texas there was an organized bolt of a large part of the Populists to the Republican party, notwithstanding its gold standard and protective tariff platform.

No campaign since that of 1860 was so hotly and bitterly contested as the "Battle of the Standards" in 1896. The Republicans broke all previous records in the amount of printed matter which they scattered broadcast over the country. Money was freely spent. McKinley remained at his home in Canton, Ohio, and received, day after day, delegations of pilgrims come to harken to his words of wisdom, which were then, through the medium of the press, presented to similar groups from Maine to California. For weeks, ten to twenty-five thousand people a day sought "the shrine of the golden calf."

In the meantime Bryan, as the Democrat-Populist candidate, toured the country, traveling over thirteen thousand miles, reaching twenty-nine States, and addressing millions of voters. It was estimated, for instance, that in the course of his tour of West Virginia at least half the electorate must have heard his voice. Most of the influential

newspapers were opposed to Bryan, but his tours
and meetings and speeches had so much news value
that they received the widest publicity. As the
campaign drew to a close, it tended more and more
to become a class contest. That it was so con-
ceived by the Populist executive committee is
apparent from one of its manifestoes:

There are but two sides in the conflict that is being
waged in this country today. On the one side are the
allied hosts of monopolies, the money power, great
trusts and railroad corporations, who seek the enactment of laws to benefit them and impoverish the people.
On the other side are the farmers, laborers, merchants,
and all others who produce wealth and bear the burdens of taxation. The one represents the wealthy and
powerful classes who want the control of the Government to plunder the people. The other represents the
people, contending for equality before the law, and the
rights of man. Between these two there is no middle
ground.

When the smoke of battle cleared away the election returns of 1896 showed that McKinley had
received 600,000 more popular votes than Bryan
and would have 271 electoral votes to 176 for the
Democrat-Populist candidate. West of the Mississippi River the cohorts of Bryan captured the
electoral vote in every State except California,

Minnesota, North Dakota, Iowa, and Oregon. The South continued its Democratic solidity, except that West Virginia and Kentucky went to McKinley. All the electoral votes of the region east of the Mississippi and north of Mason's and Dixon's line were Republican. The old Northwest, together with Iowa, Minnesota, and North Dakota, a region which had been the principal theater of the Granger movement a generation before, now joined forces with the conservative and industrial East to defeat a combination of the South with the newer agrarian and mining frontiers of the West.

The People's Party had staked all on a throw of the dice and had lost. It had given its life as a political organization to further the election of Bryan, and he had not been elected. Its hope for independent existence was now gone; its strength was considerably less in 1896 than it had been in 1892 and 1894.[1]   The explanation would seem to

[1] Of the 6,509,000 votes which Bryan received, about 4,669,000 were cast for the fusion electoral tickets.   In only seven of the fusion States is it possible to distinguish between Democrat and Populist votes; the totals here are 1,499,000 and 93,000 respectively.   The fusion Populist vote of 45,000 was essential for the success of the Bryan electors in Kansas; and in California the similar vote of 22,000, added to that of the Democrats, gave Bryan one of the electors.   In no other State in this group did the Populist vote have any effect upon the result.   The part played by the People's party in the other twenty-two of the fusion

be, in part at least, that the People's Party was "bivertebrate as well as bimetallic." It was composed of men who not long since had other political affiliations, who had left one party for the sake of the cause, and who consequently did not find it difficult to leave another for the same reason. In

---

States is difficult to determine; in some cases, however, the situation is revealed in the results of state elections. The best example of this is North Carolina, where the Democrat-Populist electors had a majority of 19,000, while at the same election fusion between Republicans and Populists for all state officers except governor and lieutenant governor was victorious. The Populist candidate for governor received about 31,000 votes and the Republican was elected. It is evident that the third party held the balance of power in North Carolina. The Populist votes were probably essential for the fusion victories in Idaho, Montana, Nebraska, and Washington; but, as there was fusion on state tickets also, it is impossible to estimate the part played by the respective parties. The total Populist vote in the ten States in which there were independent Democratic and Populist electoral tickets was 122,000 (of which 80,000 were cast in Texas and 24,000 in Alabama) and as none of the ten were close States the failure to agree on electoral tickets had no effect on the result. The "middle-of-the-road" Populist votes, in States where there were also fusion tickets amounted to only 8000 — of which 6000 were cast in Pennsylvania and 1000 each in Illinois and Kansas.

The Populist vote as a whole was much larger than 223,000 — the total usually given in the tables — for this figure does not include the vote in the twenty-two fusion States in which the ballots were not separately counted. This is apparent from the fact that the twenty-seven electoral votes from ten States which were cast for Watson came, with one exception, from States in which no separate Populist vote was recorded. It is evident, nevertheless, from the figures in States where comparisons are possible, that the party had lost ground.

the West large numbers of former Populists undoubtedly went over completely to the Democracy, even when they had the opportunity of voting for the same Bryan electors under a Populist label. In the South many members of the party, disgusted at the predicament in which they found themselves, threw in their lot with the Republicans.   The capture of the Democracy by the forces of free silver gave the death blow to Populism.

13

CHAPTER XIII

THE LEAVEN OF RADICALISM

THE People's Party was mortally stricken by the events of 1896. Most of the cohorts which had been led into the camp of Democracy were thereafter beyond the control of their leaders; and even the remnant that still called itself Populist was divided into two factions. In 1900 the radical group refused to endorse the Fusionists' nomination of Bryan and ran an independent ticket headed by Wharton Barker of Pennsylvania and that inveterate rebel, Ignatius Donnelly. This ticket, however, received only 50,000 votes, nearly one-half of which came from Texas. When the Democrats nominated Judge Alton B. Parker of New York in 1904, the Populists formally dissolved the alliance with the Democracy and nominated Thomas E. Watson of Georgia for President. By this defection the Democrats may have lost something; but the Populists gained little. Most of the radicals who deserted the Democracy at this time went over to Roosevelt, the Republican candidate. In 1908 the Populist vote fell to 29,000; in 1912 the party gave up the ghost in a thinly-attended convention which neither made nominations of its own nor endorsed any other candidate. In Congress the forces of Populism dwindled rapidly, from the 27 members of 1897 to but 10 in 1899, and none at all in 1903.

The men who had been leaders in the heyday of Populism retired from national prominence to mere local celebrity. Donnelly died in 1901, leaving a picturesque legacy of friendships and animosities, of literary controversy and radical political theory. Weaver remained with the fusion Populists through the campaign of 1900; but by 1904 he had gone over to the Democratic party. The erstwhile candidate for the presidency was content to serve as mayor of the small town of Colfax, Iowa, where he made his home until his death in 1912, respected by his neighbors and forgotten by the world. Peffer, at the expiration of his term in the Senate, ran an unsuccessful tilt for the governorship of Kansas on the Prohibition ticket. In 1900 he returned to the comfort of the Republican fold, to become an ardent supporter of McKinley and Roosevelt.

But the defection and death of Populist leaders, the collapse of the party, and the disintegration of the alliances could not stay the farmers' movement. It ebbed for a time, just as at the end of the Granger period, but it was destined to rise again. The unprecedented prosperity, especially among the farmers, which began with the closing years of the nineteenth century and has continued with little reaction down to the present has removed many causes for agrarian discontent; but some of the old evils are left, and fresh grievances have come to the front. Experience taught the farmer one lesson which he has never forgotten: that whether prosperous or not, he can and must promote his welfare by organization. So it is that, as one association or group of associations declines, others arise. In some States, where the Grange has survived or has been reintroduced, it is once more the leading organ of the agricultural class. Elsewhere other organizations, sometimes confined to a single State, sometimes transcending state lines, hold the farmers' allegiance more or less firmly; and an attempt is now being made to unite all of these associations in an American Federation of Farmers.

Until recently these orders have devoted their

energies principally to promoting the social and intellectual welfare of the farmer and to business coöperation, sometimes on a large scale. But, as soon as an organization has drawn into its ranks a considerable proportion of the farmers of a State, especially in the West, the temptation to use its power in the field of politics is almost irresistible. At first, political activity is usually confined to declarations in favor of measures believed to be in the interests of the farmers as a class; but from this it is only a short step to the support of candidates for office who are expected to work for those measures; and thence the gradation is easy to actual nominations by the order or by a farmers' convention which it has called into being. With direct primaries in operation in most of the Western States, these movements no longer culminate in the formation of the third party but in ambitious efforts to capture the dominant party in the State. Thus in Wisconsin the president of the state union of the American Society of Equity, a farmers' organization which has heretofore been mainly interested in coöperative buying and selling, was recently put forward by a "Farmers and Laborers Conference" as candidate for the nomination for governor on the Republican ticket and had the active support of the official organ of the society. In North Dakota, the Non-Partisan League, a farmers' organization avowedly political in its purposes, captured the Republican party a few years ago and now has complete control of the state government. The attempt of the League to seize the reins in Minnesota has been unsuccessful as yet, but Democratic and Republican managers are very much alarmed at its growing power. The organized farmers are once more a power in Western politics.

It is not, however, by votes cast and elections won or by the permanence of parties and organizations that the political results of the agrarian crusade are to be measured. The People's Party and its predecessors, with the farmers' organizations which supported them, professed to put measures before men and promulgated definite programs of legislation. Many of the proposals in these programs which were ridiculed at the time have long since passed beyond the stage of speculation and discussion. Regulation of railroad charges by national and state government, graduated income taxes, popular election of United States Senators, a parcels post, postal savings banks, and rural free delivery of mail are a few of these once visionary demands which have been satisfied by Federal law and constitutional

amendment. Anti-trust legislation has been enacted to meet the demand for the curbing of monopolies; and the Federal land bank system which
has recently gone into operation is practically the
proposal of the Northwestern Alliance for government loans to farmers, with the greenback feature
eliminated. Even the demand for greater volume
and flexibility of currency has been met, though in
ways quite different from those proposed by the
farmers.[1]

In general it may be said that the farmers' organizations and parties stood for increased governmental activity; they scorned the economic and
political doctrine of *laissez faire;* they believed that
the people's governments could and should be used
in many ways for promoting the welfare of the
people, for assuring social justice, and for restoring

[1] In July, 1894, when the People's Party was growing rapidly, the
editor of the *Review of Reviews* declared: "Whether the Populist
party is to prove itself capable of amalgamating a great national
political organization or whether its work is to be done through a
leavening of the old parties to a more or less extent with its doctrines
and ideas, remains to be seen. At present its influence evidently is
that of a leavening ingredient." The inclusion of the income tax in
the revenue bill put through by the Democratic majority in Congress
was described as "a mighty manifestation of the working of the Populist leaven"; and it was pointed out that "the Populist leaven in the
direction of free silver at the ratio of 16 to 1 is working yet more deeply
and ominously." The truth of the last assertion was demonstrated
two years later.

or preserving economic as well as political equality. They were pioneers in this field of social politics, but they did not work alone. Independent reformers, either singly or in groups, labor organizations and parties, and radicals everywhere coöperated with them. Both the old parties were split into factions by this progressive movement; and in 1912 a Progressive party appeared on the scene and leaped to second place in its first election, only to vanish from the stage in 1916 when both the old parties were believed to have become progressive.

The two most hopeful developments in American politics during recent years have been the progressive movement, with its program of social justice, and the growth of independent voting — both developments made possible in large part by the agrarian crusade. Perhaps the most significant contribution of the farmers' movement to American politics has been the training of the agricultural population to independent thought and action. No longer can a political party, regardless of its platform and candidates, count on the farmer vote as a certainty. The resolution of the Farmers' Alliance of Kansas "that we will no longer divide on party lines and will only cast our votes for candidates of the people, by the people, and for the people," was a declaration of a political independence which the farmers throughout the West have maintained and strengthened.   Each successive revolt took additional voters from the ranks of the old parties; and, once these ties were severed, even though the wanderers might return, their allegiance could be retained only by a due regard for their interests and desires.

BIBLIOGRAPHICAL NOTE

THE sources for the history of the agrarian crusade are to be found largely in contemporary newspapers, periodical articles, and the pamphlet proceedings of national and state organizations, which are too numerous to permit of their being listed here. The issues of such publications as the *Tribune Almanac*, the *Annual Cyclopedia* (1862–1903), and Edward McPherson's *Handbook of Politics* (1868–1894) contain platforms, election returns, and other useful material; and some of the important documents for the Granger period are in volume x of the *Documentary History of American Industrial Society* (1911), edited by John R. Commons.

When each wave of the movement for agricultural organization was at its crest, enterprising publishers seized the opportunity to bring out books dealing with the troubles of the farmers, the proposed remedies, and the origin and growth of the orders. These works, hastily compiled for sale by agents, are partisan and unreliable, but they contain material not elsewhere available, and they help the reader to appreciate the spirit of the movement. Books of this sort for the Granger period include: Edward W. Martin's (*pseud.* of J. D. McCabe) *History of the Grange Movement* (1874), Jonathan Periam's *The Groundswell* (1874), Oliver H. Kelley's *Origin and Progress of the Order of the Patrons of Husbandry* (1875), and Ezra S. Carr's *The Patrons of Husbandry on the Pacific Coast* (1875). Similar works induced by the Alliance movement are: *History of the Farmers' Alliance, the Agricultural Wheel*, etc., compiled and edited by the *St. Louis Journal of Agriculture* (1890), *Labor and Capital, Containing an Account of the Various Organizations of Farmers, Planters, and Mechanics* (1891), edited by Emory A. Allen, W. Scott Morgan's *History of the Wheel and Alliance and the Impending Revolution* (1891), H. R. Chamberlain's *The Farmers' Alliance* (1891), *The Farmers' Alliance History and Agricultural Digest* (1891), edited by N. A. Dunning, and N. B. Ashby's *The Riddle of the Sphinx* (1890). Other contemporary books dealing with the evils of which the farmers complained are: D. C. Cloud's *Monopolies and the People* (1873), William A. Peffer's *The Farmer's Side* (1891), James B. Weaver's *A Call to Action* (1891), Charles H. Otken's *The Ills of the South* (1894), Henry D. Lloyd's *Wealth against Commonwealth* (1894), and William H. Harvey's *Coin's Financial School* (1894).

The nearest approach to a comprehensive account of the farmers' movement is contained in Fred E. Haynes's *Third Party Movements Since the Civil War, with Special Reference to Iowa* (1916). The first phase of the subject is treated by Solon J. Buck in *The Granger Movement* (1913), which contains an extensive bibliography. Frank L. McVey's *The Populist Movement* (1896) is valuable principally for its bibliography of contemporary material, especially newspapers and magazine articles. For accounts of agrarian activity in the individual States, the investigator turns to the many state histories without much satisfaction. Nor can he find monographic studies for more than a few States. A. E. Paine's *The Granger Movement in Illinois* (1904 University of Illinois Studies, vol. I, No. 8) and Ellis B. Usher's *The Greenback Movement of 1875–1884 and Wisconsin's Part in It* (1911) practically exhaust the list. Elizabeth N. Barr's *The Populist Uprising*, in volume II of William E. Connelley's *Standard History of Kansas* (1918), is a vivid and sympathetic but uncritical narrative. Briefer articles have been written by Melvin J. White, *Populism in Louisiana during the Nineties*, in the *Mississippi Valley Historical Review* (June, 1918), and by Ernest D. Stewart, *The Populist Party in Indiana* in the *Indiana Magazine of History* (December, 1918). Biographical material on the Populist leaders is also scant. For Donnelly there is Everett W. Fish's *Donnelliana* (1892), a curious eulogy supplemented by "excerpts from the wit, wisdom, poetry and eloquence" of the versatile hero; and a life of General Weaver is soon to be issued by the State Historical Society of Iowa. William J. Bryan's *The First Battle* (1896) and numerous biographies of "the Commoner" treat of his connection with the Populists and the campaign of 1896. Herbert Croly's *Marcus A. Hanna* (1912) should also be consulted in this connection.

Several of the general histories of the United States since the Civil War devote considerable space to various phases of the farmers' movement. The best in this respect are Charles A. Beard's *Contemporary American History* (1914) and Frederic L. Paxson's *The New Nation* (1915). Harry Thurston Peck's *Twenty*

Years of the Republic, 1885–1905 (1906) contains an entertaining account of Populism and the campaign of 1896. Pertinent chapters and useful bibliographies will also be found in the following volumes of the *American Nation:* William A. Dunning's *Reconstruction, Political and Economic, 1865–1877* (1907), Edwin E. Sparks's *National Development, 1877–1885* (1907), and David R. Dewey's *National Problems, 1885–1897* (1907).

INDEX

Adams, C. F., candidate for presidential nomination, 15

Adams, D. W., Master of National Grange, 27

Agricultural Wheel, 116–17; *see also* National Agricultural Wheel

Aiken, D. W., on executive committee of National Grange, 27; quoted, 61–62

Alabama, Grange relief sent to, 75

Allen, Judge W. V., sent to United States Senate, 164–165, 184; quoted, 183

Alliance movement, *see* Farmers' Alliance

Altgeld, J. P., elected Governor of Illinois, 150

American Bimetallic League, 170

American Federation of Farmers, 196

American Society of Equity, 197

"American System of Finance," 80

Anthony, Susan B., speaks at National party convention, 94

Anti-Monopolist, Donnelly starts publication of, 41; activity, 86

Anti-Monopoly Organization of the United States, convention at Chicago (1884), 96; *see also* Anti-Monopoly party

Anti-Monopoly party, 31; Donnelly as leader, 39, 41; antagonism toward railroads, 50

Arkansas, Agricultural Wheel originates in Prairie County, 116; Union Labor party in, 127; fusion tickets (1896), 188

Banks and banking, *see* Finance

Barker, Wharton, radical Populist candidate (1900), 194

Barr, E. N., *The Populist Uprising*, cited, 134 (note)

"Battle of the Standards," campaign of 1896, 189

Bland, R. P., Bryan and, 179; "Father of Free Silver," 181

Brothers of Freedom, 116

Brown, B. G., elected Governor of Missouri, 14; candidate for presidential nomination, 16

Bryan, W. J., at Democratic convention (1896), 177; life, 177–78; interest in politics, 178; editor *Omaha World-Herald*, 179; in Congress, 179; personal appearance, 180; convention speech quoted, 180–81; nomination, 181, 186; and People's Party, 186, 191; campaign, 189–90; defeat, 190, 191

Buchanan, James, and National Greenback party, 82, 127

This Book may be kept

FOURTEEN

A fi